D0089337

WHAT PEOPLE ARE SAYING ABOUT
And the Bride Wore White:
Seven Secrets to Sexual Purity

Human sexuality is at the center of most of the bitter cultural struggles being waged in our day. Far too many young women don't know right from wrong when it comes to their bodies and their minds because they have bought into the low moral standards promoted on television and in contemporary movies and music. In a friendly, personal manner, Dannah Gresh helps her readers understand that sexuality is a beautiful gift from God and that He intends it to be reserved for marriage. I highly recommend *And the Bride Wore White* to any young woman who wants God's best for her life.

Dr. Richard Land, *president, Southern Evangelical Seminary, Charlotte, NC*

Dannah has a fresh way of sharing important truths we need to hear. In an age of moral decline even among our church youth, this message is needed now more than ever. Give Dannah your ear. You won't be disappointed.

Anita Lustrea, *author, speaker, radio personality*

I admire Dannah Gresh in so many ways. Her ministry is moving; her writing is relevant; she is a role model to women of all ages and seasons of life. As a survivor, speaker, and author on the topic of sexual abuse, I constantly see and hear firsthand the pain of the sexually broken and I understand the deep need for Dannah's message. The rerelease of her bestseller *And The Bride Wore White* is an answer to the cry of our culture. This book is a timeless classic that will bring healing and hope to all generations.

Nicole Bromley, *speaker and author, oneVOICEenterprises*

I first read *And the Bride Wore White* when it was an unpublished manuscript and I was a freshman in college. I devoured it in a single setting, and the lessons I learned made a huge impact on my life. As a woman who has now been married more than a decade I still remember and cherish the lessons Dannah presents in this book. Dannah does what other authors do not by moving beyond God's call to purity and outlining a plan to make waiting possible and desirable. This book gave me the blueprint to build a pure marriage, a gift that I am eternally grateful for. Consider *And the Bride Wore White* a must-read for every girl who's ever dreamed of a pure and holy marriage.

Erin Davis, *author of* Beyond Bath Time

The loss of virginity is not simply a physical state of being, but affects the emotional, mental, and spiritual lives of every girl—which is why I appreciate Dannah Gresh and her passion to see girls not only value their virginity but why they ought to do so. With vulnerability, humor, and grace, this book provides girls with the tools they need to take ownership of their bodies, minds, and hearts.

Crystal Renaud, *author,* Dirty Girls Come Clean

I cannot think of any book more beautifully inspiring than *And the Bride Wore White*. My daughters loved Dannah's insights, her humor, and her call for a life without regrets. I am deeply grateful for the realistic role model she is for my daughters. . . . She has changed their lives, and in doing so she has changed mine.

Tammy Maltby, *author*

What a pleasure it was to read this book. . . . Dannah helps walk us down the aisle of a pure lifestyle!

Leslee J. Unruh, *president, National Abstinence Clearinghouse*

This book is a great field guide for any teenager who wants to become serious about sexual purity and rise above the defeats of the past.

Greg Stier, *president, Dare 2 Share Ministries*

AND THE Bride Wore White

SEVEN SECRETS TO SEXUAL PURITY

Dannah Gresh

MOODY PUBLISHERS
CHICAGO

© 1999, 2004, 2012 by
DANNAH GRESH

All rights reserved. No part of this book may be reproduced in any form without permission in writing from the publisher, except in the case of brief quotations embodied in critical articles or reviews.

All Scripture quotations, unless otherwise indicated, are taken from the *Holy Bible, New International Version*®, NIV®. Copyright ©1973, 1978, 1984 by Biblica, Inc.™ Used by permission of Zondervan. All rights reserved worldwide. www.zondervan.com

Scripture quotations marked KJV are taken from the King James Version.

Scripture quotations marked NKJV are taken from the *New King James Version*. Copyright © 1982 by Thomas Nelson, Inc. Used by permission. All rights reserved.

Scripture quotations marked NLT are taken from the *Holy Bible, New Living Translation*, copyright © 1996, 2004, 2007. Used by permission of Tyndale House Publishers, Inc., Wheaton, Illinois 60189, U.S.A. All rights reserved.

Scripture quotations marked NASB are taken from the *New American Standard Bible*®, Copyright © 1960, 1962, 1963, 1968, 1971, 1972, 1973, 1975, 1977, 1995 by The Lockman Foundation. Used by permission. (www.Lockman.org)

Edited by Cheryl Dunlop
Interior and cover design: Julia Ryan / DesignByJulia.com
Cover Image and chapter photos : J&A Photography
Author Photo: Steve Smith

All websites and phone numbers listed herein are accurate at the time of publication but may change in the future or cease to exist. The listing of website references and resources does not imply publisher endorsement of the site's entire contents. Groups and organizations are listed for informational purposes, and listing does not imply publisher endorsement of their activities.

Library of Congress Cataloging-in-Publication Data

Gresh, Dannah.
  And the bride wore white : seven secrets to sexual purity / Dannah Gresh.
    p. cm.
  ISBN 978-0-8024-0813-6
  1. Sexual ethics. 2. Sex--Biblical teaching. I. Title.
  HQ32.G617 2012
  176'.4--dc23
                        2012010904

We hope you enjoy this book from Moody Publishers. Our goal is to provide high-quality, thought-provoking books and products that connect truth to your real needs and challenges. For more information on other books and products written and produced from a biblical perspective, go to www.moodypublishers.com or write to:

Moody Publishers
820 N. LaSalle Boulevard
Chicago, IL 60610

5 7 9 10 8 6

Printed in the United States of America

To my princess, Lexi

When I first wrote this you were toddling around
and just getting your legs. Now you are about
to use those legs to leave us. I couldn't be more
proud of the woman you have become. You wear
embroidered garments interwoven with gold.

To my China doll, Autumn

When I first wrote this you were far from me.
Now you are near to my heart. Thank you for
becoming my daughter. You are God's princess.

"All glorious is the princess within her chamber;
her gown is interwoven with gold.
In embroidered garments she is led to the king."
PSALM 45:13–14

Contents

250,000 Lives Later

Satan bullies us when our hearts begin to follow God's prompting in such a way that we will strengthen the kingdom of God. In the midnineties I began to mentor two girls—Lauren and Erin—in my little hometown and to take small handfuls of girls on weekend-long purity retreats. Each time I shared my

testimony about sexual pain and God's restoration and healing, I would endure several days of such taunting in my spirit and my head that I felt physically sick. My heart palpitated. I was restless, kept awake by penetrating arrows of lies. "You're such a hypocrite! Let this message be given by someone who won't ruin the cause of Christ." "Who do you think you are? If they knew the real depravity of your sin, you'd never accomplish anything." "Remember your past!" "You sound like such a fool when you talk about that!"

Finally, I began to quote truth. One verse was worn out in my mind. "God does not give me a spirit of fear, but of power and of love and of a sound mind." The jeering stopped. Period. End of taunting! It was just the beginning. *Two hundred and fifty thousand lives* later, God is still prompting me to tell my story and to speak the truth about sexual purity to today's beautiful women of God.

I am grateful to those who helped me bring the first edition of *And the Bride Wore White* to you. They include Deb Haffey, Dennis Shere, Greg Thornton, Jim Bell, Bill Soderberg, Cheryl Dunlop, Dave DeWit, Julia Ryan, Dan Seifert, and many faithful friends such as my my mentors Tippy Duncan and Ramona Taylor.

As I am working on this, the third edition of *And the Bride Wore White*, I'm so thankful to Eileen King, my faithful assistant, and Mike Keil, my manager. And after twelve years, I'm still enjoying the wonderful work of Julia Ryan, the publishing industry's most extraordinary designer. Suzie Rothgeb and Jacqueline Gardner helped me edit this revised edition and I am *so* grateful.

My models for this edition included Justine Addleman, Chizuruoke and Maru Anderson, Autumn Gresh, Lexi Gresh, Adam and Meagan Jepson, Maggie Jepson, Sue Jepson, and Kalkidan Streit.

But as always, those who've been there for every up and every down are my beloved family. Mom and Dad have given up time, money, and warehouse space to let this little dream grow! Bob, my hero and lover, has rearranged his life as the message of this book increases. Lexi and Autumn, my faithful twins separated at birth (pretty literal in this case) are patient and supportive as I write book after book. Robby, however, once best verbalized my family's love and support. As I shared with him for the first time how I had sinned and been forgiven, I asked him if he was disappointed. "In what?" he asked as if I hadn't just poured my heart out to him. "In the fact that I'd once messed up like this," I said. He had one simple, loving, forgiveness-filled response.

"Mom, we all mess up. That's why Jesus died."

And so it is!

Embrace that as you read this work of God's hand in my life.

I am living in His great love!

Dannah

and the
bride
wore
white

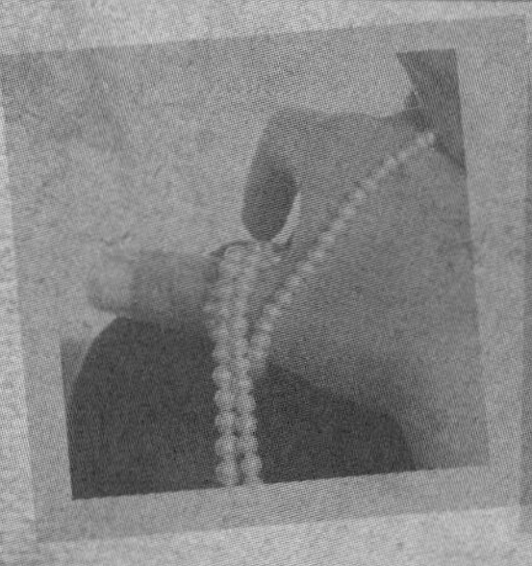

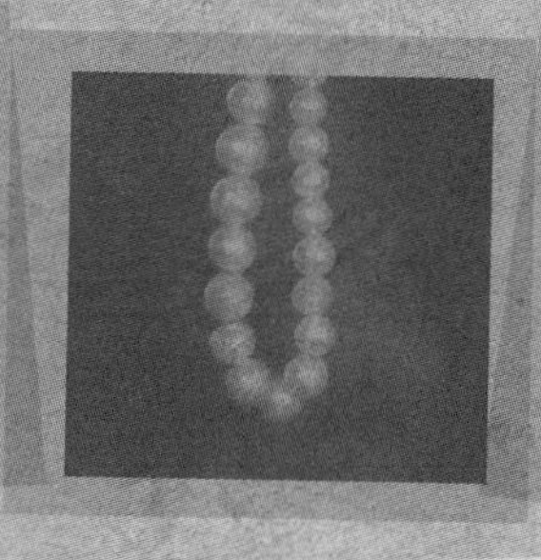

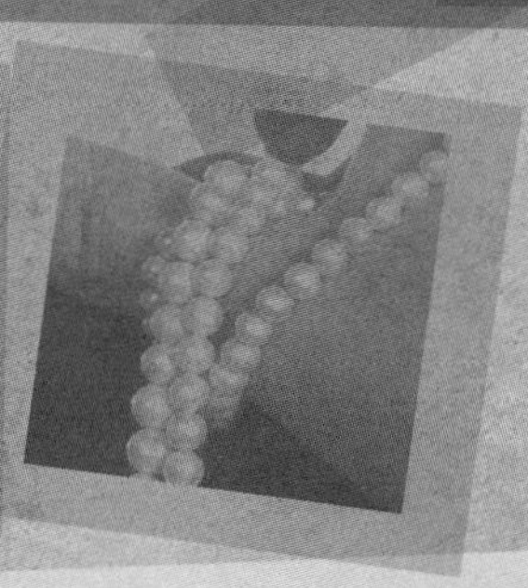

Deciding to Live a Life of Purity

By the time I was fifteen, my copy of *And the Bride Wore White* had been underlined, earmarked, and highlighted. I was the poster child for purity, had kissed dating goodbye, and was saving my first kiss for my wedding day…at least, that was the plan. But by the age of twenty-two, curiosity got the best of me and I gave my first kiss to some guy I met one night…then never saw again.

Foolishly convinced that I had lost my purity and couldn't get it back, I began walking away from my Father's house, metaphorically speaking. I exchanged rules for "freedom" and distracted myself from my shame with unholy choices. I walked deeper into sin, stifling my Father's words that played over and over in my head. Eventually I found myself at the end of a string of selfish decisions, barely hanging on to the fine line that was my virginity. Days later, crumpled onto my bedroom floor, crying unquenchable tears, I glimpsed that old copy of *Bride* tucked away on my bookshelf. As I read Dannah's familiar words for the hundredth time, I decided I had enough. I wanted to go home. Bracing myself for condemnation, I slowly began walking the road to my Daddy…and with great joy, He ran down the road to welcome me back.

He not only delivered me from my shame but also set a crown of dignity on my head! I am His redeemed bride, His prodigal daughter, His beloved ra'yah, and He has a holy calling on my life. In what could only be an ironic twist of grace, I began interning for Dannah's ministry, Pure Freedom, the next year, despite the fact that I'd failed. But I suppose that's the point, isn't it? That we have all failed. That God's mercy is deeper than our deepest sin. That purity isn't something we can lose, it's something we can walk toward. And that our heavenly Father is ever so patient as we learn how to take our first steps.

All we need to do is start walking. So here's my hand…let's brush off our scraped knees and help each other up. Let's walk home together, sweet sister of mine. Our Father is waiting for us!

Jacqueline Gardner

and the bride wore white

Deciding to Live a Lifestyle of Purity

[God's grace] teaches us to say "No" to ungodliness and worldly passions, and to live self-controlled, upright and godly lives in this present age, while we wait for the blessed hope—the glorious appearing of our great God and Savior, Jesus Christ. (Titus 2:12–13)

T*he day I met the man who would become my husband, he* had just returned from Florida, where he and the rest of the varsity tennis team had spent spring break practicing endlessly. His white teeth contrasted sharply with the deep tan and his dark hair. His nose was peeling just a bit as he began to flirt with me. That profile of his cheery countenance is etched in my mind forever.

On my wedding day and at my request, his tan was there to contrast with the clean white shirt and bow tie we had chosen for him to wear under his long black tails. He was the man of my dreams, and this day was a fairy tale come true. And me? I wore a white hand-beaded dress with a nine-foot train. I marched across fresh rose petals as violinists, stretched along both sides of the sanctuary, played the wedding march. At the front of the sanctuary, we faced our guests so that they could see the joy on our faces as we exchanged vows. The kiss was sweet and simple, ending with a knowing glance. There would be more time for tenderness that night.

At the reception, guests munched on hors d'oeuvres as an orchestra played in the background, pausing only for the announcement from the master of ceremonies, "Ladies and Gentlemen, our bride and groom have arrived. I present for the first time in public Mr. and Mrs. . . ." I was a Mrs.! Applause filled the room as the strains from the orchestra ushered us to our head table. I waltzed beautifully with my father, who returned a bow to my groom a few minutes into the waltz. As my new husband and I started to dance, we succeeded in royally ruining the graceful presence my father had established, but it didn't matter. We were the prince and princess of the ball, and anything we did would charm the guests.

Hours later, the princess found herself locked in the bathroom of a honeymoon suite, trying to decide how to make her grand entrance. (If I had it to do over again, I would claim the room for myself and lock him in the bathroom to decide when and how to enter!) Was it too soon for the lacy negligee? Were the full-length satin pj's too modest for tonight? Should I put my hair up? Would it seem too vain to freshen my makeup? We had not discussed lights—would they be on or off when I came out? In the end, I opted for the modesty and the vanity. (And hoped the lights would be low!)

But when my eyes met my husband's deep blue ones . . . full of compassion and true love . . . the nervousness was replaced with a knowing. We had waited. We had made it through the maze of temptation, and now a warm and comforting Presence was with us, assuring us that this covenant into which we were about to enter would be blessed.

And the blessing was more than we had hoped for.

How did we make it? God knows that I was not perfect. How did I wait for the wonderful gift of being one with a man I so tenderly loved? Well, it's a wonderful, romantic story that includes moments of critical decisions . . . some I am proud of and some I wish I had made differently. I am going to share it all with you. Through it I learned seven special secrets that gave me the strength to make it through a lot of temptation.

It all started with the truth of Titus 2:12–13. Those verses say that God's grace does not automatically keep us from worldly passions. In all of your love for God, you could be blindsided by worldly passions. When I realized how difficult the path of purity can be, I stood before God and I said, "OK, teach me to say no. I know these worldly passions exist, but I know the only way I will be able to say no is if You teach me!" And from that moment on, God worked in me and gave me a resolve that I did not even know that I could have within me. The path . . . and the waiting . . . were much easier. The difference was that now I had placed myself in God's presence to be taught how to say no to worldly passions.

If you didn't go to class, your teacher could not fill you with all of the knowledge that he or she had to give. The God of the universe won't teach you either, unless you place yourself in His presence. I have been praying for you. I want so desperately for you to stand before God and to ask Him to teach you to say no to worldly passions so that you can live a self-controlled, godly, upright life.

You cannot attain purity all on your own.

I cannot unveil to you some formula of protection.

Your parents cannot tell you something that will keep you innocent.

Only God can do that!

Won't you stop right now and ask Him to teach you as you read this book to say no to worldly passions?

WRITE YOUR STORY. Now, here is the most important part of this book. You need a journal or notebook to really make this book change your life. You see, it's not what I write that is important and can protect your purity. It is what you write that will knock Satan between the eyes.

Get out your journal and write a letter to God. Explain to Him where you are in your struggle to stand pure before Him. It could be any area of your life—sexuality, substance abuse, language, anger—anything that is causing heartache in your life. Give each part of your history over to Him. Tell Him you are sorry if you have failed. Pray that He will keep you shielded from worldly passions. And specifically request Him to be your teacher while you are reading this book.

Go ahead. Write!

I have prayed for you and for this very moment in your life.

If you feel God telling you to ponder what you've written or what you have heard Him saying, then just be quiet for today, but come back soon! You and I are going on a complete journey of our sexual lives—that is, yours and mine. For me, we're going to go back a few years, and I am going to tell you about some of my most intimate moments—some shameful and some quite beautiful. For you, we are going to build a complete godly vision of your love life to come. Let's go!

MY STORY

As you will soon see, not every choice I made about my sexual purity was governed by God's plan. I never dreamed of having a ministry to encourage young girls to treasure their purity. God pushed me into doing my very first purity retreat when a conflict arose in my church over whether or not a junior in high school should attend a women's retreat dealing with sexual healing. Since I was a corporate trainer, the women of the church asked me to put together a purity retreat specifically for the junior and senior high girls. I have to admit, my pride pleaded with the Lord for another assignment, but I eventually gave in. I did not share any of myself on that first retreat, but I saw women who did, and I saw how incredible the response was to how "real" they were. I cautiously walked into the arena of exposing myself and found junior high, senior high, and college-aged girls who were incredibly challenged by my story, much to my humility. It made them eager to explore God's heart on the matter of sexuality. And so, I offer you my story in these pages. It has been rewritten through meticulous retrieval of my memory through sixteen years of diaries and journals. I present it in a narrative format at the beginning of each chapter. Not one detail written about within these pages was made up. They were all carefully recorded within my journals. God must have known they would be used for this book.

CELEBRATION STORIES

Laced throughout this book are many short stories about friends I have known for years or have met at my purity retreats. A few are noted as "Celebration Stories" for the great work God has done in their life through this very book! In many cases, I use just a first name or I have changed the name to protect the person's privacy or the privacy of someone else who may have been involved in the person's story. Most of these stories were submitted by the young women who've lived them. A few are my favorite memories from the past few years!

CHAPTER TWO

Satan's big fat

sex lies

CELEBRATION STORY

Sarah Marinau on Journaling

I actually picked up the book And the Bride Wore White *after my school friend had recently gotten married and given birth to her first child just five months after the wedding.* The title made me think of my friend who was a Christian but had obviously given up some of the standards she believed in. I read the book, and not only did I not want to put it down, but I also started a prayer journal in which I learned to pour my heart out to my Lord and Savior Jesus Christ. It was such an encouraging book. Whenever meeting a girlfriend, I would ask, "Have you read *And the Bride Wore White?*"

Sarah Marinau, Australia

Sarah went on to host a princess party at her house for younger girls aged 13–20. She has become a "burning flame"!

Satan's big fat sex lies

Learning to Recognize the Truth

The devil ... was a murderer from the beginning,
not holding to the truth, for there is no truth in him.
When he lies, he speaks his native language,
for he is a liar and the father of lies. (John 8:44)

H*ot, thick air engulfed the camp where I had gathered with* dozens of other Christian teens to be trained as a "summer missionary." We would be spending the summer teaching Bible classes in underprivileged neighborhoods. We eagerly dug into stacks of visual aids and endless pages of mandated Bible stories, hoping to impress our teachers, who would rigidly scrutinize our delivery and memorization.

Laying my chin down on the picnic table, I pondered the others studying among the trees.

Good thing I'm not lookin' for guys here, I thought, reflecting again on the near absence of them. *Anyway, I've got the greatest guy of all waiting for me at home.*

I reached into my pocket for the letter, which I'd already read a dozen times. I hoped another letter would come today. As if God were monitoring my distracted devotion, thunder rumbled in the distance.

Moments later, the clouds burst suddenly and quickly flooded the tiny stream that ran through the camp. Dozens of us frolicked and romped in the water up to our hips. We played football, tackled one another, and floated in the gentle current as the fresh June rain poured onto the ground and into our spirits.

When the sun authoritatively returned, our soggy clothes suddenly weighed us down, and we gave in to the cries of our sponsors to come inside. As I stepped onto the dorm steps, Jenny gasped. I looked at her with a raised eyebrow.

"You're bleeding," she said, pointing to my foot.

Lifting my foot, I could see a small piece of glistening glass.

"Doesn't hurt," I assured my tenderhearted friend as I pulled the glass from my foot.

Within hours, I had a red line climbing my leg—the beginning of blood poisoning. Much like an undiagnosed, growing deadly cancer, it did not hurt. I spent the next twenty-four hours soaking my wound to extract the poison.

I did not know it at the time, but that day would be a portrait of the next few years of my life. Those years would prove that the most blissful moments often have deadly potential—even if it doesn't hurt at first.

I was channel surfing and was stopped dead in my tracks by a program called *Guys and Sex*. It was a string of interviews with young men talking about sex. I was intrigued. I have often wanted to get into the heads of guys to see what they were really thinking.

Two handsome brothers seemed to be the hunks and sexual bravadoes of the program. Their shoulder length, wavy hair gave them a casual-yet-finessed Orlando Bloom sort of look. They spent the nights prowling for women. Their goal? To have a new "lover" every evening. And with their looks and charm, they did.

They talked of their conquests with laughter and freedom. They were having fun. But the last take was what intrigued me.

As they sat in a hot tub sipping beers, the interviewer asked, "Do you think you'll ever marry?"

The brothers laughed. "Yeah, whatever," said one.

"Doesn't everyone?" boasted the other.

"But, seriously," pushed the interviewer, "will you marry?"

The laughter stopped. One set his beer down and ran his fingers through his hair nervously. He then looked pensively into the distance.

"Yeah, but not for a long time," he said.

"Who will you marry?" asked the interviewer.

"Not any of these girls," he spoke with assurance. "I want my wife to be pure."

The beauty of sexual love is being camouflaged by big fat lies. That, of course, is because Satan has entered onto the scene. John 8:44 tells us the true character of Satan. The devil "was a murderer from the beginning, not holding to the truth, for there is no truth in him. When he lies, he speaks his native language, for he is a liar and the father of lies." What is Satan? He is a big fat liar. And I think his favorite lies relate to your sexuality because of its powerful symbolism. (We will talk more about that later. For now, know that the true meaning of sex is so far beyond the pitiful meaning this world offers that it'll blow your mind if you've never heard about it!)

I like to compare the way he lies to you and me about sex to the way he lied to Eve about the Tree of the Knowledge of Good and Evil. Why? God's Word tells us that everything in the garden of Eden was created by God's own hand. It also tells us that He is incapable of making anything that is not good. So, it is very possible that the Tree of the Knowledge of Good and Evil would have had quite an interesting and noble purpose had Eve simply *waited* for God to reveal it to her in His time. Interesting thought, don't you think? My friend, sex is like that. It is such a good and wonderful thing that God has created *if we wait* for God's timing to enjoy it. Satan knows that one of the most beautiful things in our world is the sexual union between a husband and a wife when they wait to enjoy it after their wedding. He wants to rob you of that, so he lies to you.

I think he told those brothers on TV that it would give them power and fulfillment. But you can tell that deep down they have some sense of the deception. Why else would they need so many conquests?

He told my friend Aimee that a sexual relationship with her boyfriend could heal the pain she felt from not having a good relationship with her dad.

He told my Christian friend Jennifer that she would lose her boyfriend if she did not provide for some of his sexual needs—though she told him she would not have sex with him. He raped her.

He told my Christian friend Leeza that if she did everything but actual inter-course, she was still "pure."

When I was fifteen, he told me that I was protected in a strong Christian dating relationship. I did not feel that I needed to be watchful. I lost a great deal of my innocence through that deception.

HPV:

To vaccinate or not to vaccinate?

Since HPV is the only known cause of cervical cancer, pharmaceutical giants have done something to address it. This is no small thing. Cervical cancer is the second most common cancer in women.

In recent years, a vaccination that protects a sexually active young woman against 4 of about 100 strains of HPV is not only available, but there's a lot of pressure to get it. While two of the strains the vaccine protects against are responsible for about 70 percent of cervical cancer, two strains the vaccine does not confront are responsible for the remainder of cancer cases. So, it does not provide guaranteed protection. At the same time, abstinence does. A woman who is not sexually active will never acquire HPV.

I haven't been quick to get on board, but you have to make the decision with your parents after a lot of prayer and research. A major concern of mine is that the vaccine has only been tested for four years before release, so we have no long-term outcomes concerning risk. And, there have been unusual side effects ranging from fainting to muscle weakness to death that cannot be proven to be related to the vaccine, but those who experienced them are begging for further investigation.

The only no-risk method of protection against HPV is abstinence, followed by faithfulness in a lifelong mutually monogamous marriage relationship.

One of Satan's lines is "everyone is doing it." What a lie! Not everyone is doing it. In recent years, only 46 percent of high school students surveyed had engaged in sexual intercourse.[1] That's a majority who haven't!

Here's another big fat lie that he has made many well-intentioned parents believe: the risk of sexually transmitted infections is so great that we have no choice but to throw the option of "safer sex" at them. Satan decided there were not enough teenagers sacrificing their innocence, so he came up with a grand scheme. He got their parents to think, *If everyone is doing it, and there is something awful like AIDS out there, I had better give my kids tools to do it safely*. Now he has parents and mentors saying, "We hope you don't have sex, but if you do, use a condom!" What a double message.

Satan's lie is that to keep you safe, we have to equivocate on our message. In truth, I'm not offended at the thought of teaching teenagers about contraception, any more than I'd be offended about factually presenting other issues in an anatomy and physiology class. I am offended that we water down our resolve to encourage you to live a life of purity and abstinence in the process. So-called, safe sex is one of the most dangerous activities that exist.

Chlamydia is the most common sexually transmitted disease circulating today.[2] If you get it, it's unlikely that you'll ever even know you have it. Only a minority ever experience telltale symptoms…until it is too late. At that point, many women who have it experience pelvic inflammatory disease, which leads to infertility. No babies. Ever.

A condom will help to prevent chlamydia, but not all the time. Hope this isn't TMI, but there are thirteen steps to using one of the things correctly. The end result is that they have a controversial failure rate in preventing *any* sexually transmitted infection. You can research it yourself on the Internet to see how varied the estimates are, but I'm going to go with the conservative estimates that they fail about 50 percent of the time. Those just aren't good odds when you're talking about the risk of never having babies.

The human papilloma virus (HPV) is another common viral STI. It is so common that at least 50 percent of sexually active people get HPV.[3] HPV is incurable and can be uncomfortable and embarrassing—it sometimes causes genital warts— but more important it is recognized that HPV is the only cause of cervical cancer.[4] While other factors may make the risk of cervical cancer greater, HPV is considered "necessary" to acquire this type of cancer.[5] Guess how much protection a condom provides against HPV? None. HPV is not spread by bodily fluids but by intimate skin-to-skin contact. How safe is that? It simply isn't safe at all.

Know this, friend! Satan looks at your sexuality much like he did Eve's Tree of the Knowledge of Good and Evil. He is threatened by it and will do anything to see that you misuse it.

Of course, Satan uses many lies, and he customizes them each time to be just right for the person to whom he is lying. But as I listen to women tell their stories about their road to purity, I hear three distinct lies that Satan tends to use. They are much like the lies he told Eve in the garden. I want you to know what they are so you can see them when he throws them your way. Here comes the first of Satan's biggies!

WRITE YOUR STORY. What do you think? How has Satan deceived you? Wait! Before you think that you have not been deceived, think about it for a moment. Ask God to reveal to you anything of which you might not be aware. (I was not aware of my deception. It was a clever one!) Even if you hold strongly to your innocence and you desire to walk down the wedding aisle innocent, pray that God would reveal to you what part in your heart needs to be challenged and purified. This is very important. Take time to write your search and your prayer out to the Lord in your journal.

Satan's biggest, fattest sex lie

CELEBRATION STORY

Jana Hekalová on Passion for Purity

My name is Jana Hekalová. I come from the Czech Republic, a city called Pardubice. I am a high school teacher, but I also do part-time youth ministry and training. Years ago, I spent a month in the States, in Colorado. There I bought the book *And the Bride Wore White* and the leaders' guide. I am involved in girls' ministry in our church, and for quite a while I had been thinking about how to introduce the topic of sex and dating into my pastoral care in a more organized way. I held my first retreat in April 2002, and since then I have started organizing retreats and training female leaders all over the country.

Jana Hekalová, Czech Republic

(For information on how to obtain retreat materials, see the back of this book.)

Satan's biggest, fattest sex lie

Resisting the Lure to Sin

"Hey! Don't you know God is withholding a good thing from you?"

Now the snake was the best liar of all the animals that God had made. He said to Eve, "Hey, did I hear God say, 'You can't eat from any trees in the garden'?" Eve answered, "Oh, we can eat from the trees in the garden but God did say 'You must not eat from that tree in the middle of the garden. Don't even touch it or you will die.'" "Oh, you won't die," lied the snake. "Come now, God knows that when you bite into that fruit you will be so full of knowledge. Why, you'll be just like God, knowing good from evil." So Eve looked at the tree and noticed that it was full of fruit and beautiful. Suddenly she believed it would give her wisdom. So she took some and ate it. She also gave some to Adam, who was standing right beside her, and he ate it. (Genesis 3:1–6, author's paraphrase)

I sat dazed in the corner of the classroom. The recruiter who had encouraged me to be a summer missionary the previous summer was here to tell the junior class at my Christian high school about being a summer missionary.

As she began to talk, my mind wandered off to the previous June, to summer missionary camp. I was walking down the concrete camp pathway. I joined the circle of other new graduates, and we sang, "I've got joy, down in my heart . . . deep, deep down in my heart! J-O-Y down in my heart." I did have joy. My love for Jesus was so intense that it gave me butterflies to think of the little children who awaited my Bible stories that summer.

Over the summer, dozens of young lives placed their hearts in Jesus' hands. Every Wednesday, I was true to the contract that I had signed as I spent a minimum of one full hour in prayer for my ministry and the ministry of the other summer missionaries. Sometimes I grabbed the phone and called one of them. We were so close. God had developed an awesome bond of friendship between us. Once, one of the neatest guys at the camp called me . . . and we prayed over the phone for each other's ministry and for God's protection . . . zzzzzzzrip . . .

I was on another path, and I wasn't feeling protected. It was October and I was walking down a pathway in the woods with Michael. We were alone. I wanted to be with him, and yet I didn't. The past few months had been a labyrinth of temptation, and I could not find the way out. His desires were ones I could not identify with as he groped and grabbed at me every chance he had. I was like a deer in oncoming headlights. I did not know how to respond. I wanted him to stop forcing his desires upon me, yet they had awakened other desires within me. I wanted to belong to him and to be wanted by him. Whenever he'd write to me—oh, those letters wove webs around my heart. And he always expressed so much of a desire to serve God together. I mean, look at him—he is good, and he is good for me. I could control him. Kisses, cuddles . . . just innocent touching. I could control him. But at the end of that path I found how very out of control I was . . . zzzzzrip.

"Dannah was a summer missionary last summer and is going to share some of her experiences with you," my recruiter said, ripping me back into the room. She also brought me back into the miserable reality that I had forfeited what really was a good thing for something that only looked like a good thing, but that had turned out to be a lonely, imprisoning act of sin.

If you didn't read all of Genesis 3:1–6 (on the previous page) because you know the story, go back and read it again.

Verses 4 and 5 are where Satan dealt a literal deathblow to Eve. Notice how he first appealed to her intellect, making her feel inferior by saying, "Oh, you won't die . . . come now, don't *you* know that God knows you will be just like Him when you bite into that fruit?" He talked as if he had experience. Do you know what I think? I think that even Satan, like Adam and Eve, knew nothing of what death meant. After all, when would he have seen it? I think only God knew what the full consequences would be.

Satan was basically saying, "Hey, don't you know God is withholding something good from you? I know how truly good it is and that it really won't hurt you at all but will make you just like God."

He caused Eve to believe that she had the intellect to draw her own morality—or to determine what was right for her. Oh, if only Eve had stood firmly on the truth of what God said. He said, "Of the tree of the knowledge of good and evil *you shall not eat,* for in the day that you eat of it you shall surely die" (Genesis 2:17 NKJV, italics added). God said no, and Eve should have too. Instead, she decided she was smart enough to debate the devil. And because Eve was busy talking, he found her weakness . . . touch. She had told him God said they couldn't even touch it. Perhaps that gave him an idea. "Oh, you won't die," hissed the snake as he slithered around the ripe fruit, tempting her to reach out to "just" touch it.

Today, Satan still loves to make you feel inferior, like you are missing something and can't measure up. He likes to make you think that you cannot possibly wait for this wonderful gift, and that if you're really intelligent about it, you shouldn't have to wait. Eve's story sounds so much like the sexually enlightened world in which you and I live. We're constantly being thrust into debate over sexual issues. But, as Ed Young reminds us in *Pure Sex,* "All that the current experts have managed to give us in terms of sexual enlightenment has not satisfied our longing for something transcendent, something pure and beautiful. Instead, we've settled for what some have called 'nutra-sex'—artificial substitutes for pure sex that eventually cause cancer—both in relationships and in the soul." [1]

Oh please, stand firm . . . firm . . . firm on God's Word. Ephesians 5:3 says that within the church, "There must not be even a hint of sexual immorality, or of any kind of impurity." Paul says, "But not everything is good for us. So refuse to let anything have power over you. Don't be immoral in matters of sex. That is a sin against your own body *in a way that no other sin is*" (see 1 Corinthians 6:12, 18, italics added).

God says "No!" and you can too! No debating. Just "No!"

Sometimes, if you have enough resolve, Satan whispers into your ear, "You don't have to go all the way. Just try a few little things. That won't hurt."

Oh no! Here comes that "touch" again. It seems Eve is not the only female to throw that into the debate.

I told you before that my friend Leeza believed the lie that if she just did not have intercourse, she would be pure. Leeza was one of the most gorgeous girls I have ever known. Her hair was long and a natural rich chestnut color. Her facial features were dainty. She was a catch, and the guys knew it. She dated anyone, but leaned toward the athletic playboys. They would date her for a while, get as much as they could from her sexually, and then drop her because it wasn't enough. So she really got around.

Toward the end of our college years, Leeza really began to regret her lifestyle. She realized that she now had a reputation that would follow her the rest of her life. It would be difficult to return to her tiny hometown without running into a guy who had a sexual memory of her.

In my last few years of college, I saw a lot of friends who had guarded their virginity through the toughest years suddenly give in to testing their sexual performances right before their wedding or even before they became engaged. Most of them were remorseful of their choice. Several got pregnant.

I can't fail to mention something: oral sex. About 63 percent of young women aged fifteen to twenty-four have had oral sex.[2] And many of them believe themselves to be pure. This is how they "touch" sex, thinking themselves virgins. Technically, I guess, they are. But then again, they don't call it "oral friendship," do they? It's sex.

There are even ways to "touch" without literally touching anything. Approximately one in three teenagers have admitted to sexting—sending nude or semi-nude pictures via text message.[3] And plenty of young women feel that it's no

 big deal to post sexy or provocative profile pictures of themselves on Facebook. They figure it's a way to get all of the attention and none of the consequences. But even that "touches" sex.

Regretfully, my own innocent "touching" gradually escalated into a form of "nutra-sex." I can tell you that it left a painful cancer that I thought might never be cured. I fell for Satan's lie that God was withholding something really great from me.

God's truth includes the fact that there are practical reasons to wait. One of the most credible sexual studies undertaken to date was made available to the public by the University of Chicago. Some of its findings prompted these statements:

- "People who reported being most physically pleased (by sex) and emotionally satisfied were married couples."

- "Lowest rates of satisfaction were among men and women who were neither married nor living with someone—the very group thought to be having the hottest sex."

- "Physical and emotional satisfaction started to decline when people had more than one sexual partner."[4]

Guess what? God's Word promises that very thing in Deuteronomy 6:24 when it says, "The Lord commanded us to obey all these decrees . . . so that we might always PROSPER!" The writer was talking about the laws God had just given. He was explaining that the purpose of them was to make the nation of Israel prosperous. I see that trend throughout Scripture. God desired for Israel then, and He desires for you and me today, to live strong, healthy, prosperous lives. God does not withhold anything from us to frustrate us. He knows how much more glorious sex will be if we wait. Let me say this one more time. God says "No!" and you can too. No debating. No touching. Just "No!"

I'll tell you a few more secrets about prospering in God's truth later on. First, I have to tell you about the second big lie and how I fell for it, because the first one and the second one usually hit hard and fast. You cannot fully understand the impact of the first without understanding the sting of the second.

NOWHERE

"There is a dullness, monotony, sheer boredom in all of life when virginity and purity are no longer protected and prized. By trying to grab fulfillment everywhere, we find it nowhere."[5]

Elisabeth Elliot
Passion and Purity

Satan's second big fat sex lie

CELEBRATION STORY

Sandi on Hiding

My family has always courted. I'm sad to say that even
though my family had this value established to protect
me, I lost my virginity when I was fifteen. I decided never
to marry. God had called me to be a missionary in a very
specific and remote location in Africa. I would serve Him
there as a single woman. I didn't court again until I was a
senior in college. My dad asked me to agree to court a
guy. I did it just so I wouldn't have to tell my dad about my
past, I figured the relationship would fizzle, but it didn't.
Imagine my shock when weeks later my suitor told me
that God had put this tiny little remote location in Africa
on his heart to reach for Christ—the exact place I'd been
praying for all these years. Soon this man I'd come to love
in just a few months asked for my hand in marriage. I ran
away crying. Surely I wasn't worthy. Hours later, my suitor
found me and simply said, "I know why you feel unworthy.
It can only be one thing. I forgive you and I would like
to spend my life helping you to live in that forgiveness.
I feel the Lord wants me to give you two weeks." Exactly
two weeks from that day I was sitting in a purity retreat
I'd been drug to by my friends. Dannah Gresh was the
speaker. I felt God's healing flood my heart as I talked to
her that day. After she prayed for me, she asked me, "So,
what about that marriage proposal?" I just smiled and said,
"I'm going to say yes!"

Sandi

Satan's second big fat sex lie

Hiding Behind the Fig Leaves

"Ha! Now that you've fallen, God has no use for you!"

Then Adam and Eve suddenly realized they were naked and they sewed fig leaves together to cover themselves. Then the man and his wife heard the sound of God walking nearby in the garden in the cool of the day, and they hid behind some trees. And God called to Adam, "Where are you?" He answered, "I heard You and I was afraid because I was naked, so I hid." God said, "Who told you that you were naked? Have you eaten from the tree I told you not to?" Adam said, "It was the woman You gave me. She gave some to me, and I ate it." Then God said to Eve, "What have you done?" Eve answered, "It was the snake. He deceived me and I ate it." (Genesis 3:7–13, author's paraphrase)

Each night was the same. I walked along a dark, busy highway with Michael. Horns blared. Lights glared, and yet the darkness was thick. Aside from the busy highway, I couldn't see anything but blackness.

I held my boyfriend's hand more tightly. I turned to look at him. I called his name.

He quickly looked away, avoiding my gaze. I called him again.

Why wouldn't he look at me?

Suddenly a great shaft of light dropped from the sky and loomed authoritatively in front of us. It had a warm golden glow, which contrasted sharply against the coldness of the rest of this place. My boyfriend quietly pulled his hand from mine, and I felt him step behind me. The great light was directly in front of me.

I did not hear a voice, but I felt as if that shaft of light was the presence of God inviting me to step into it—to choose God instead of this earthly love that I wanted to turn and cling to. I hesitated just long enough for the light to vanish as quickly as it appeared. I turned around, and my boyfriend was gone.

The highway was empty.

The darkness engulfed me.

I was alone.

"No!" I screamed, waking from my deep sleep.

Blue moonlight reached into my bedroom and created a shaft of light across my bed. I looked into it and scrunched deeper into the blankets, heavy with a cold sweat.

How many times in the past months had that dream awakened me from my restful slumber? It was like no other dream I had ever had. It was real, and every detail was memorable. There was meaning in it. My pain was so great.

I inched deeper and deeper into the covers and hid in my cold sweat.

The man who is now my wonderful husband was a resident assistant in college. Once he walked into a unit to check on things late Saturday evening. He heard weeping coming from a closet. Opening the door, he found a guy curled up in the closet. That man wanted to be left alone in that closet, but he was an emotional wreck.

After lengthy consolation and trying to determine what could possibly have driven a healthy, strong man to hide in his closet and wail, an admission came. The young woman he had been dating and hoped to marry one day had finally agreed to have sex with him. They did. And now he was hiding, uncertain as to whether or not he could repair the disrespect he had shown her and himself.

Sound familiar? Sort of like what Adam and Eve did after they bit into that fruit. Oh, my friend, I can tell you that they did not hide lightly. They hid with a great sense of grief and guilt. I know from experience.

In choosing my boyfriend I lost the awareness of the very presence of God whom I once so loved. It was a lot like Adam and Eve's experience. It wasn't that

God wasn't there. He was walking nearby, saying, "Where are you, Dannah?" I was too ashamed to come out. I resigned from teaching Sunday school. I quit my job as a summer missionary.

I hid.

I can just see Satan off in the corner laughing, "Ha! Now that you've fallen, God has no use for you!" It took me a very long time to realize that was a big fat lie! (Oh, to have those years back!)

What's the truth?

Before I get to the bottom line, let me first say there is no escaping the consequences of sin. Adam and Eve, because of their sin, were kicked out of the garden. Adam had to work hard to feed his family, and Eve would experience great pain in childbirth. Even the snake lost his legs. The consequences were tough.

King David truly sinned—he had sex with another man's wife (Bathsheba). Then, because he got her pregnant, he ended up killing her husband to hide his sin. Some pretty tough consequences, really. There's an illegitimate baby on the way and blood on David's hands. I bet David and Bathsheba both had a lot of sleepless nights. I can picture Bathsheba greatly mourning the loss of her husband's life because, in a way, it was her fault. And later when the child died, I can see them both thinking about the fact that they would never have known that horrible loss had they not sinned together.

Yes, the consequences of sin can last a long time and be very painful, *but does that mean that God no longer wanted David to be in a loving, lasting relationship with Him?* Well, God watched the whole soap-opera-like drama unfold, and He sent Nathan to confront David. (My guess is that David was in the place where you think you have to work your way back into God's heart—wipe the slate clean and *then* come before God.) When David was confronted, he repented, and Nathan immediately said, "The Lord has taken away your sin" (2 Samuel 12:13). There was no hesitance, no delay. God immediately welcomed David back into His presence. And He did continue to use him. David will forever be honored as "a man after God's own heart!" (see 1 Samuel 13:14).

Did his sexual sin mean that God had no use for him? No!

Satan likes to make you feel as if your sin has ruined you and will stick with you forever. The truth is that God picks up that sin and hurls it as far as the east is from the west. He promises us in Ezekiel 18:22 that "none of the offenses he has committed will be remembered." Believe that. Know the truth of God. And crush Satan's lie with it.

For a long time I felt as if my sexual sin was my ultimate destruction. I had forsaken God's plan and made a lesser choice. My heart got tangled up, and now I was paying the consequences. I felt lonely in the midst of what should have been a fun relationship. I felt trapped during years when I should have been feeling free and enjoying my singleness. I felt ashamed to enter into God's presence.

Ever *feel* something like that? Yours may not be necessarily sexual in nature. Maybe you are just *consumed* with the idea of having a boyfriend. Or your language robs you of your testimony. How do you release it so that you don't feel utterly useless in God's hands or useless in general?

Let me try to bring the classic writing of the great author C. S. Lewis into today's lingo. In *The Great Divorce,* he writes about a slimy red lizard clinging to a certain ghost. The lizard taunted and teased that ghost, whispering great lies to him every day. The ghost tried to control the lizard, but it was not successful.

An angel appeared and offered to rid the ghost of the little lizard. But the ghost understood that to be relieved of the beast it would be necessary to kill it. The ghost just didn't have the heart for that.

That's when the rationalizations began. The ghost thought he might train and tame the lizard. He thought perhaps he could release it gradually. The angel insisted the gradual approach would not work, as this little red lizard was a very good liar. It was either the death of the lizard or the defeat of the ghost.

Finally, the ghost gave the angel permission to remove the lizard. The lizard screamed as it was twisted from the shoulder it clung to. With one great twist of the wrist, the angel sent it directly to the ground, where the impact broke its back. Then an amazing thing happened. The ghost suddenly became a perfect man and the limp, dead lizard was transformed into a very-much-alive silver and gold stallion. The new man leaped onto the great horse, and they rode off into the distance.

As the Teacher in Lewis's book explains, "What is a lizard compared with a stallion? Lust is a weak, poor, whimpering whispering thing compared with that richness and energy of desire which will arise when lust has been killed."

Up until the age of fifteen, I never doubted God's ability to lead me and use me. During the course of my relationship with Michael, that confidence was shattered into a million pieces. I was not able to pick up those pieces because a little lizard on my shoulder was whispering the most horrible things into my ears. "You cannot break up with him. Don't be a hypocrite. Come on. You won't do that again. What will you tell your friends about why you broke up? Oh, you might want to stop teaching Sunday school until you get this little thing worked out and, by all means, don't even think of teaching Christian clubs. It's not that you're really bad, but what kind of an example would it be if you were found out? You need to save those jobs for the truly pure in heart."

I want you to know what I did not know when I was trapped in my sin. I acted so much like Adam and Eve did when they took that forbidden fruit. I hid. I felt as if God had no use for me now that I had fallen. Yes, there were consequences. But just as God walked through the garden lovingly looking for His dear Adam and Eve, He was eager to bring me back into a loving relationship with Him. He was like that angel, just waiting to break the neck of that little, lying lizard, lust. I was just not having much luck getting the nerve up to give Him permission.

WRITE YOUR STORY. What about you? What's the name of the little lizard in your life? Lust? Outright sex? Heavy petting? Boy craziness? Language? Bingeing and purging? Anger? Materialism? Stop right now and visualize that little slimy lizard on your shoulder. Then look directly into the eyes of God, who can free you from it and just say, "I'm helpless here. What comes next?"

Go ahead. Grab your journal and write about it. Please do it.

breakin' up

is hard to do

Elizabeth Urbanowicz on Breaking UP

After twelve years of praying for the man I would one day marry, I began to get to know a wonderful, loving, godly man. He was a man who I knew loved the Lord more than he would ever love me, who was committed to serving his Savior, and who loved me enough to honor my conviction to save my first kiss for my wedding day. After nine months of dating, and on the exact day he was planning to propose, the Lord revealed that this young man was and for many years had been in bondage to sexual sin. I was heartbroken, scared, ashamed, and completely confused. How could God have allowed our relationship to progress this far when He knew I was being deceived? Why was my dream of a loving, pure, Christ-centered marriage being torn from me?

The following months were long and painful. But God was slowly, patiently, and ever so faithfully working in my heart and my mind. In times of loneliness and despair, He held me as I poured out my grief through tears. In times of anger and resentment, He taught me how to truly forgive through the saving power of His cross. In times of sadness and heartache, He taught me to receive His peace through giving thanks in all circumstances. I learned that even in those moments of absolute brokenness I could depend on Him, He was always there.

Even though it was painful, I'm so glad our relationship ended when it did. And I have hope for the future.

Elizabeth Urbanowicz, pictured here with her dad

breakin' up
is hard to do

Breaking Off Sinful Relationships in Three Steps

*Throw off your old evil nature and your former way of life,
which is rotten through and through, full of lust and deception.
Instead, there must be a spiritual renewal of your thoughts
and attitudes. You must display a new nature because
you are a new person, created in God's likeness—
righteous, holy, and true. (Ephesians 4:22–24 NLT)*

J "Just look at this," I said, irritated with my lack of self-control. "My
journal is full of it. Break up . . . make up . . . break up . . . make up."

I handed my journal to Lisa Payne, pointing to the most
recent set of entries.

*1-23 . . . It's over. Michael and I told each other we loved each
other several times. And I know we do. I know this is right,
but it doesn't take the hurt away.*

*1-24 . . . We are together again. Crazy, huh? He called at
midnight last night and we "worked it out."*

1-26 . . . My spiritual condition has only worsened. I want to be in God's will, but I'm only halfway there so I'm not at all there.

Lisa closed the journal and gave me a penetrating glance. In that split second we both remembered that breakup that had happened ten months previously. We had spent that night sitting together crying and holding each other.

She had recently lost her father to cancer. I felt like I'd lost my heart to a spiritual cancer. In our individual pain, we had felt the other person's pain. I remembered telling her how stupid I felt crying over a stupid boyfriend when her pain was caused by a much more significant loss.

"Hey, at least I have someone to bawl with," she had sniffled, passing me a new box of tissues. We both laughed that really great, freeing laugh that only comes to visit in the midst of a good, long cry.

Then hours later he had called. We'd gotten back together, and I felt really rotten for leaving her alone in her moment of pain, while I waltzed back down the easy road.

"Well," she said, snapping me back to the present. "You know what you have to do. Break this relationship off for good. I'm not going to make this easy for you this time."

Lisa was always saying, "Personhood before partnership!" It was her dating motto, and a good one at that. My relationship was clearly one that put partnership before my own personal development and, unfortunately, my relationship with God.

"You're a great friend," I said sarcastically. I reached for the telephone. It seemed as if it took an hour for my heavy hand to reach the receiver. I dialed his number, then looked at Lisa. She was standing at the door ready to leave, offering me a few moments alone to do what needed to be done.

"Hello," said the warm, familiar voice that I felt belonged to me.

"Hi," was all I could get out.

"What's wrong?" he said, reading my voice without hesitation.

I was silent.

"Dannah," he said, pleadingly.

How I love to hear him say my name, I thought. *Maybe I can talk to him for a few minutes first . . . absorb the last few moments of "us."*

"Dannah!" he pushed.

"It's over," I said coldly, like a child releasing an animal back into the wild, knowing only a cruel release would send him off. "I do not want this anymore. Our relationship is not what God wants for our lives right now," I said. "You have got to let go too."

He was silent. He'd never been silent before. I believed that his desire was also to live within God's blessing, and he understood that meant ending our relationship.

After a few moments, we both quietly hung up the telephone. I reached for my journal to cry out to my God as tears fell silently down my cheeks.

11-20 . . . My heart is cold and numb. I mean it's so intense I feel an actual heaviness in my chest. Lord, in Your heavenly plan, what are You teaching me? How long does it take? My will crosses Yours. My will has to die.

Lisa had come back. She wrapped her arms around me, and I collapsed into them. We cried again. This time, he didn't call back.

I f you have given your heart or your body to someone, and you have been feeling a twinge of discomfort as you've read the past few chapters, that is probably the Holy Spirit speaking to you. As I write this, I have been asking Him daily to work in *your* life! Is He? Well, you can be 100 percent sure that if He is, it is because He has an awesome plan for your life. It is even greater than what you could possibly imagine. I know you think this guy is the love of your life. You cannot see down the road yet. You cannot see anyone even coming close to this young man, but God has a plan that is soooo much better.

Right now, you have a tough decision to make. It doesn't matter if you've dated for one month or five years or if the relationship became sexual or it was just squeezin' in on your love life with Jesus, breakin' up is hard to do!

But Scripture is clear over and over again that we *must* walk away from anything that hinders our love for God. The verse above says to "throw" off your former way of life. I know that is not easy. I really cannot make the process less painful for you, but I can give you a step-by-step plan for walking through it.

1 TELL **GOD**

Right before I broke up with my boyfriend, I had gotten into the Word of God. God gave me the strength and conviction to make right choices. He was so tender about it too.

The book of Ezekiel paints a very ugly picture of how hard-hearted Israel had been toward the God who loved them and who considered Himself Israel's Lover. At one point, God told Ezekiel to describe Israel as a helpless, bloodied newborn left lying in a field with the umbilical cord still hanging from it when God showed up to lovingly clean it, clothe it, and care for it. (Kind of gross, huh? But God really wanted us to see in that picture that He would love us no matter how He found us.) Then as Israel grew to become a woman, she took God for a brief moment as her Love.

GOD CAN
Reach the Pain

I know that breakin' up is hard to do. I know the pain is something no one else can seem to reach. Understand that God can. "Bare heights of loneliness . . . a wilderness whose burning winds sweep over glowing sands. What are they to Him? Even there He can refresh us. Even there He can renew us."

Amy Carmichael, *Windows*

Then she proceeded to take the wonderful garments, jewels, and gifts her Love had made her and give them to her other lovers. This caused great hurt to the God of the universe as again and again Israel chose to love everything but Him. In Ezekiel 11 this great, patient Lover said, "It's time to come back to Me." But how would Israel ever accomplish that? She had had children with her other lovers. She had memories, houses, possessions as a result of her other relationships.

Israel's True Love showed up with a great gift in Ezekiel 11:19 when He said, "I will give them an *undivided* heart." Verse 20 goes on to say, "*Then*, they will . . . be careful to keep my laws. They will be my people, and I will be their God" (italics added).

He knows you have memories. He knows you have possessions, songs, and nicknames. He understands how terribly painful breaking up can be, and He wants to hold your heart in His hands and cause it to be *undivided* so you can go through with it. He does not expect you to prove yourself back into His heart by doing this tough thing without Him and *then* coming into His presence. *Start* by talking to God and receiving His gift of an undivided heart.

What exactly do I mean by an undivided heart? Of course, I am speaking of your heart figuratively, as we often do when we talk of love and devotion. The figurative heart is the central "organ" of your emotional and spiritual life. Let's compare it to the physical heart, which is the central organ of your physical life. When someone's heart is healthy, the four chambers beat in rhythm. What would happen if half of the heart decided it wasn't feeling much like working with the other half? You might have palpitations, or your heart might skip a beat. It could hurt a lot, or you could barely notice it. It would not be an immediate death sentence, but your body would become weaker and weaker if that half of the heart kept resisting the responsibility to do its job in conjunction with the other half. Eventually, that "divided heart" would ruin the quality of your life, and it might one day actually kill you.

Our figurative hearts are like that. I hope that, like me, there was one day when you sat before the great, loving God of the universe and said, "OK, I'm not perfect. I sin. That makes me unworthy of being in Your presence. I know I really deserve death, but thank You so, so much for sending Your dear Son, Jesus, to die in my place. I accept the precious gift of eternal life through His death. From now until eternity, my heart belongs to You!" From that moment on, your figurative heart's job is to pump in tune with the heart of God. But if the side of your heart that handles the emotions gets caught up in an ungodly or distracting relationship, pattern, or habit, you've got the same condition as you would if your physical heart were beating out of sync. Your emotions, spiritual drive, and the quality of life suddenly begin to ebb away. Your figurative heart simply cannot stand to beat out of rhythm any more than your physical heart can.

2 TELL A **FRIEND**

Just because God begins to work in you does not mean your human heart won't find it very difficult to stay on course. I couldn't have broken up with my boyfriend without Lisa to bear the load with me. She was a very important element in regaining my strength to live a lifestyle of purity.

I suggest you find one or more friends to shoulder the burden for two reasons. They can test what you are thinking and they can enCOURAGE you—or give you courage—to stay on course. You need to talk to that friend before you call your boyfriend and give him the chance to pull on your heartstrings.

I still do this in my life. Mostly, I go to my husband and say, "This is what I feel God telling me about this. Can you encourage me?" I also use other wise counselors such as my mother and older godly women to borrow courage. This past week, a special senior-higher in my youth group broke up with her boyfriend. She needed to do it, but it was very painful. So she told a Christian friend. The friend encouraged her and suggested she write a letter to the guy so she could have everything thought out and so that she could not be sweet-talked out of her commitment. Then the friend told her to make a copy of the letter to keep and to go back to for courage in the weeks to come. It was good advice from a good friend.

Tell a friend what you sense God saying so that you can test it and so that the friend will enCOURAGE you to go through with it.

3 MAKE A **FAST**, STRATEGIC **EXIT**

I wish we could ask Joseph about Potiphar's wife. She was one of the richest and most popular women in Egypt. I bet she took Egyptian mud baths and had her feet waxed to keep off the dust. Come to think of it, she probably never walked through the dust. They probably carried her around Egypt in some kind of gold-plated seat. I envision milky skin and jet black hair in that classic Egyptian cut. In fact, she may have started that hairstyle craze. Do you get where I'm going? I think she was a hot item! But in Genesis 39, Joseph didn't think twice about running . . . and fast.

If you have a relationship that provides you with the temptation to sin or that simply distracts you from your love for God, it needs to be discontinued immediately. Joseph is a great example of a man who knew how to make a fast, strategic exit.

I am very proud of a girl named Lana. She was a brand-new, baby Christian when she came to my retreat. Her current boyfriend had introduced her to Jesus. At the retreat, she admitted that there was pressure in the relationship to be physical despite the fact that they both loved God so much. The day after the retreat she broke up with him. Now that's a fast, strategic exit that would have impressed Joseph. Guess what? Shortly after the retreat her "ex" got a girl pregnant. He had to quit college to get a job. That could have been Lana, but it wasn't.

Where do you stand with this issue of breakin' up? Is there a relationship you have had in the recent past that still causes pain? Go to God for an undivided heart and find a friend to give you courage. Are you still in a relationship that needs to be ended? Start with an intense talk with God and beg for that undivided heart, then find a friend to borrow courage and make that fast, strategic exit. Maybe you are not in or have never been in a relationship that needs to be cut off. Bravo! The seven secrets are just around the corner, and they can help you never have to make this choice.

> Repent, then, and turn to God,
> so that your sins may be wiped out,
> that times of refreshing may
> come from the Lord. (Acts 3:19)

IT'S YOUR TURN: WRITE YOUR STORY. Take a moment and beg God for an undivided heart. Even if you don't have a relationship right this very moment but you are consumed with a desire to be with a guy, you must begin to ask for this undivided heart. Go to God. Tell Him about the memories, the hopes, the dreams. Ask Him for an undivided heart.

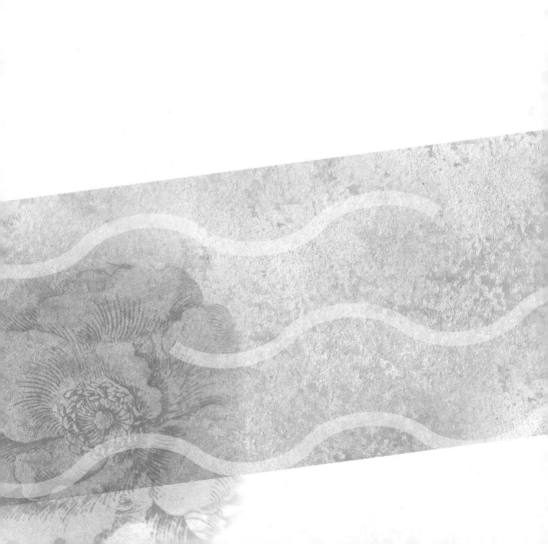

SECRET

1

purity is
a process

Naomi on New Beginnings

I was always curious about sex. It was never talked about at all in my house, which only served to fuel my interest. An interest turned into an addiction after I found pornography and raunchy romance novels on the Internet. I even started to masturbate. After about a year I finally woke up and realized how bad my addiction was getting and decided I needed to stop. I tried and tried but would always go back to that one website or read that part of the book one more time. I knew God wouldn't want me when I was living in sin so I told myself that I'd start taking God seriously once I had these addictions under control. But all of my efforts failed and I felt so alone. One day I thought, *What's the point? Why should I keep living?* I can still hear the devil's words telling me that if I took the pills, all of my guilt and pain would go away. By God's grace I instead dropped to my knees and began to weep. The God of the universe came and wept with me on that floor. I felt His tender, loving-kindness and I knew deep in my heart that He still loved me. As I started to walk with God again, He started shedding the layers of bondage and abuse. I still struggle and some days I'm very close to caving in but there's a difference. I no longer rely on my own strength but on His strength in me.

Naomi

purity is
a process

Defining Innocence and Purity

[God desires] that you may **become** *blameless and pure."*
(Philippians 2:15, emphasis added)

H "*Hey, Dannah!*" *called Jim, a blond, muscular college student* *I'd recently met.* I walked over to meet him. He said, "John, Dan, and I are gonna grill some steaks for dinner right now. You game? It's on me."

If he was asking me out, I wasn't ready. If he was just being nice, I didn't want to impose. I had stayed in Cedarville for a few weeks of the summer to finish the yearbook. In this tiny town, it was common courtesy for summer students to hang together since there wasn't much to do.

I juggled the stack of files I was carrying to my left hip as I fumbled for my keys . . . and for a response.

"Well, actually I just ordered a pizza for myself. I should probably be here when it arrives, don't you think?" I laughed.

Cool response, Dannah, I thought. *Didn't reflect your discomfort at all. Good line.* And it was true. The pizza was on its way.

"Maybe next time," said Jim with a wave as he walked away.

The truth was, I wasn't so sure about getting back into the dating arena. For now that meant avoiding guys altogether since I knew my tendency was to cling to one if I had the chance. I had really blown it before, and I was having a lot of fun being single. I was going to have a game plan next time. I wasn't ready quite yet.

Down in the yearbook office, I pulled my journal and my Bible out of my sack. My yearbook office had proven to be a quiet respite with God over and over again. I read through some of the entries of the past year.

> *9-15 . . . I yearn for someone to hold me . . . to make it better. I want to back up and change time and make everything perfect. Why me, Lord? Why have You chosen me to know the things I have known? Can I make a difference? There is a thick layer of dusty secrets on my heart. Only You can know them. Only You can reach within and wash it away . . . only You.*

I reached for my pen and my Bible. I felt quite different now. I was sitting before the great God of the universe, and He was teaching me to say no to worldly passions and to live a lifestyle of purity. I began to write:

> *I am pure! The Lord has completely purified me. 1 John 2:28; 3:1–3: "Now, dear children, continue in him . . . confident and unashamed. . . . How great is the love the Father has lavished on us. . . . When [Christ] appears, we shall be like him. . . . Everyone who has this hope in him purifies himself, just as he is pure."*

May I ask you something? Do you ever feel as if you've totally missed the mark? Like you've messed up the perfection that God started with when you were born? Like you have contaminated the goodness He created in you? Maybe it is something small and silly that makes you feel inferior. Maybe it's a huge secret, a sexual sin that keeps you cowering in your walk with God. Memories can be more convicting than any judge or jury.

I went through a real period of struggling with my own purity at the beginning of my college years. I thought I had completely blown it. Memories came back to haunt me and make me feel inferior. In my mind, I was no longer pure. I had ruined the perfection God had created in me. Let's test that against Scripture for a second . . . "Surely I was sinful at birth, sinful from the time my mother conceived me" (Psalm 51:5).

"All have sinned and fall short of the glory of God" (Romans 3:23).

"There is not a righteous man on earth who does what is right and never sins" (Ecclesiastes 7:20).

OK, you weren't born yesterday, so you can handle this . . . *you weren't born pure.* You were innocent when you were born, but Scripture says you were born sinful. So this notion that you have "lost" your purity is nonsense. You never had it.

I love the way Kaye Briscoe King, an author and a Christian counselor, looks at this whole issue.[1] She has developed The Journey Spiral (see illustration) upon which she says we "travel" our life's journey, hopefully ending in the dead center of the spiral where we have become truly Christlike. (Stick with me on this. It gets a little deep, but this knowledge is really freeing.)

See that line wiggling across the bottom of the graphic? That represents you

The Journey Spiral

Adapted from "Journey: Wolfing into Wholeness: Body, Mind and Spirit," by Kaye Briscoe King.
Modified and simplified for this book.

or me before we knew Christ Jesus as our loving Lord and Savior. The moment we commit our lives to Christ and accept His precious blood as payment for our own sad, sinful nature, we begin the exciting journey toward becoming Christlike. That's the first step toward becoming pure, since Christ was pure in every way. I feel very strongly that without Jesus it is not possible to live a lifestyle of purity. I know young women who have some yucky stuff in their past but whose lifestyles exude purity. And I know young women who think they are pure in a very technical sense but whose lifestyles are anything but pure. Innocence is where you begin, and it is possible that you have lost some of your innocence, but purity . . . that's where you end up!

The characters that cross the spiral represent the sins we repeatedly struggle with. Let's name just one—Lust. Each of us was born with Lust hanging around. The dude was sitting there waiting for us to get to him. When we choose to journey toward a close relationship with God (and more often when we do not), he rears his ugly head.

One of three things will happen when you meet Lust. You'll breeze past him with God's help. Or he'll taunt and tease you pretty effectively, maybe causing you to sin, but you eventually struggle past him. Or you get stuck there with him for a long, long, long time.

Hopefully you make it past him and say, "Whew! Made it." And you journey on. But suddenly one day, you notice (because you are walking in a spiral) that there he is again. He doesn't look quite as scary because you have seen him before and God helped you win the battle with him then. So you tell him, *No way! I fought with you before. You're a part of the past.* But there he is and you have to go on.

This happened to me not long ago. At 11:00 at night, I let myself get fooled into thinking that I needed to watch a popular television show, believing it was "research" for this book. (The show had a sexual theme.) That show got me feeling desires, thinking thoughts, dreaming dreams that were not OK. While guys often struggle with visual temptation, I find that most of the time you and I are more prone to simple, emotional fantasy. It doesn't seem sexual to us at all because it doesn't include sexual thoughts or sexual touching. But our hearts are wrapped up in giving ourselves to someone. That's where I was that night. A dangerous place to be.

Since my husband was on a trip, I crawled into bed alone, and I thought, *I am either going to fantasize myself to sleep or I am going to tell Lust no!* I mumbled, "God, I'm too sleepy to fight this off. Help me, please! I have seen this monster before, and he doesn't look so big and scary anymore, but I could easily play his game tonight." I reached for the nearest book, forcing my mind to read rather than think, and I soon fell asleep. The next day, I admitted it to my mom and felt really great for not giving in to Lust. (See that pattern? Tell God, Tell a Friend, Make a Fast Strategic Exit—which for me was reading some boring poetry.)

The good news is that each and every evil dude we face on our journey can (like C. S. Lewis's little red lizard) be completely transformed. As you make right choices and follow the pattern to tell God, tell a friend, and make a fast, strategic exit, that wimpy little beast turns into something wonderful for God. It becomes the character that God originally created to dwell within you but that was marred and manipulated when sin entered into the world . . . and into you and me. As you confront Lust and make right choices with the help of God and friends and lots of fast, strategic exits . . . that little monster, Lust, slowly becomes God's originally created, contented, uncompromised companion—Purity.

I felt so relieved when I first had the Spiral explained to me. You see, I felt guilty for always running into Lust. He was smaller and his roar less threatening each time, but he kept showing up. The fact that he showed up to taunt me, I learned, was not my sin—it was a given and a chance to walk deeper into the spiral and closer to my dear God *if* I said "no" to Lust. Purity is a process. What a freeing secret . . .

- I was not born pure.

- I will face the beast of Lust, perhaps over and over again, but that in itself is not a sin. Rather it is a chance to develop my purity by talking to God, talking to a friend, and making a fast, strategic exit.

- I can *become* pure.

I think it is extremely important that you grasp this. Understand that you are going to run into this guy Lust someday. Be ready for him and know that saying no to him is what pushes you in that direction toward purity.

Understanding that purity is a process is the first secret toward living a lifestyle of purity, but it is just head knowledge. You need practical how-to skills to get you there. So keep reading. The next secret is not only very practical but also a great deal of fun.

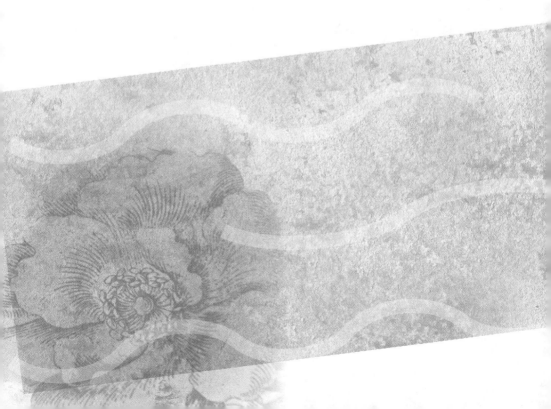

SECRET

2

purity dreams

of its future

CELEBRATION STORY

Melanie on Her Wish List

*I thought that God wanted me to stay single forever . . .
don't ask me why. When I read Dannah's book, I loved
it, but when it came to writing a "wish list" about the
man of my dreams, I first refused. "God, how can You
ask me to dream about something that You might
never give me?" But finally, after fighting and crying a
lot, I wrote a list and set it aside, not knowing if I was
ever going to see my wish fulfilled. Two years later, at
thirty years old, I am getting married to a wonderful
man who didn't quite seem at first sight to "fit the list."
But as I got to know him as a friend first, I've been
able to see that he was just who I needed.*

Melanie, Ontario, Canada

purity dreams of its future

Envisioning a Godly Husband

*Though one may be overpowered,
two can defend themselves. A cord of three strands
is not quickly broken. (Ecclesiastes 4:12)*

In ten minutes, Chad, a very handsome college junior, would be picking *me* up. Already he had treasured me that night, as if I was a real princess. He took time to give me all the details of his careful plans. He found out that I really like Chinese food and was planning to take me to a very special Chinese restaurant.

Before I knew it, we were discussing his volunteer work as a counselor at a crisis pregnancy center while we sipped green tea.

"All of the girls are a little shaken when they first come in," he said. "But we test them to verify if they are, in fact, pregnant. Missing a menstrual cycle does not necessarily mean they are pregnant. I am always relieved when I can tell them it is negative."

Wow! I thought. *Did he just say "menstrual cycle"? This guy is confident and sensitive. He's not afraid. I like that.* As I ate my chicken and peanuts, he told me more about what he felt was his calling in the field of psychology.

"You are so sure of what you want to be," I said, amazed at his clear vision. "I'm still struggling with whether or not I like my major."

"Give it time, Dannah," he encouraged me. "You've got almost three years to go. I'm nearly finished. I am supposed to know by now."

After dinner, we went to a nearby college campus to watch a movie being shown on the campus lawn. We sat under the stars on a blanket relaxing together among hundreds of other college students. There wasn't any pressure to be near each other. He made me feel comfortable.

"I have something very special planned for dessert," he said as he wrapped the blanket under his arm. He had a really neat way of making everything seem special. Well, no, he had a really neat way of making *me* feel special.

He drove me to a bakery where he knew the ladies who were baking. I could tell that he came often and that they loved him. After carefully selecting our pastries, he took me to his apartment, where he introduced me to his roommates and then banished them to their rooms while he made homemade hot cocoa for us. We ended the night sipping the cocoa, which was accompanied by equally delicious conversation.

The next day, he wrote *me* a thank-you note for the wonderful evening.

Though it was one of the greatest dates of my life, the next day I had come to a sure conclusion.

I heard my mother's voice as if she were standing next to me, "Dannah, dating is not a game. It's not about casually playing with someone's heart. If you don't intend to marry him, don't date him. Know what you are looking for and only date the guy who fits that dream."

The day she had told me that, I'd written what I called a "shopping list for HIM." My words on this rugged piece of rose-colored stationery drew a picture of the man of my dreams. Chad was a perfect fit spiritually, meeting my dream of a man with a deep commitment to God who deeply desired to serve Him with whatever career he chose. He was obviously physically fit and handsome. (I remembered giggling with Mom when we wrote "must have cute buns" on my shopping list. We'd left it on the list because it was a memory of our conversation and because physical fitness was important to me.)

But Chad fell short in the personality category. Oh, he had a *great* personality, but he was too much like me. I believed I needed someone who could make me laugh since I was always more prone to "being productive" and "getting my work done." Chad was a productive guy and would one day have a successful career. I was certain of that. That was his one and only "flaw."

I politely turned down his offer for a second date the following Saturday. I spent the night in my dorm room with a cup of instant hot chocolate, thinking how lucky the girl who married Chad would be.

We live in a world of instant gratification. Want a snack? Pop the microwave open. Want to message a friend? Pop up your Facebook account. Want a tan? Pop into a tanning bed.

It has been said that one of the main reasons teens today are having sex is because they "can't visualize the future." Can you visualize your future? When you close your eyes, do you see the man you will marry?

If you aim for nothing, you'll hit it. Is that how you want to aim for your husband—with an open, blank slate? Or do you want to dream of someone who is just right for you, who complements your weaknesses, and who fulfills your hopes and desires?

That was my choice.

And from the moment I wrote my "shopping list for HIM," I never dated a guy for a second time unless he met the criteria on that list. Each one got one chance for me to measure him against the list.

I liked it that way. It took away a lot of the guesswork as far as when to say yes and when to say no, and it didn't give me a chance to hurt him or him a chance to hurt me.

What about you? Do you have a dream? Is he tall, dark, and handsome or blond, rugged, and woodsy? Does he have a lot of drive to be business minded, or is he a nine-to-fiver who can't wait to clock out to come home to be with you?

It's time to build a vision of your husband-to-be and a vision for how you will honor him on your dates—all of them, not just the ones with him.

HIS LIST

Is your character what it ought to be? Are you letting your true personality shine through when you are around guys, or are you putting on a show? Have you taken the time to build some goals and vision for your future? Above all, would he know just by being around you that your faith is strong? How would you measure up if the man who is waiting for you were dreaming of you right now? (He might be, ya know!)

WRITE YOUR STORY

THE **LIST**: YOUR **DREAM**

This is one of the really fun parts of this book. Grab a bowl of popcorn, your favorite drink, a pen, and your journal. You can even grab a friend to do this with you. It can be a lot of fun. Now, close your eyes and dream.

THAT **PHYSIQUE**!

What does he look like? Write it down. Does he work out? Does that matter at all, or not? Does he have short or long hair? Is he unconcerned with his appearance? Is he natural and carefree? Do you see his attractiveness better through his heart than through his physical appearance?

Have fun with this section. Don't hold anything back. But remember to take it lightly. Be willing to be flexible with what you think he should look like. Write it down. Dream, my friend, dream!

PERSONALITY PLUS!

What is his personality like? If you are not sure, look at your relationship with your girlfriends. Which ones work best and have turned out to be long lasting? Be careful here and get some advice from friends and family. I really let my mom help me here. She pointed out that my best friends were outgoing, humorous, and energetic even though I am more quiet, reserved, and steady. So my husband probably needed to be more crazy and humorous to balance my personality. (And he certainly is!)

It is vital at this point to think through some character qualities that you would require such as "honest" and "committed" and "hardworking." Though they may seem like givens, you will run into guys who don't have what you might expect everyone should have in the character department. I include character issues under "Personality Plus" because it seems to me that personality is often influenced or at least controlled by character or the lack of it.

One thing to consider when you start using your list is that the outer personality can sometimes hide the true character of a guy. On my "shopping list for HIM," I wrote, "Honest and full of integrity to the point that he even shares with me the bad things. I will love him more if I know what they are and where I stand." My husband's character is deep. He wants to be vulnerably honest. He is easily hurt when someone lies to him or when so-called "friends" desert him.

THAT **PHYSIQUE** _____

_____

_____

_____

_____

_____

PERSONALITY PLUS _____

_____

_____

_____

_____

HIS **DREAMS** _____

_____

_____

_____

_____

HIS **OTHER** LOVE _____

_____

_____

_____

_____

He simply expects that everyone is honest and full of integrity. This part of his character sometimes causes his usual, frisky, puppylike personality to become quiet and pensive. I did not see that until many, many months into our relationship. He is proof that the most difficult category to "measure" may be "Personality Plus" if you are looking for character.

Dream, my friend. Dream. Write.

HIS **DREAMS!**

What does he dream of becoming . . . of doing with his life? Is it compatible with your dreams for yourself? (It would not work very well to fall in love with someone who wants to be a lumberjack and live on a mountain with ten kids, if you dream of a high-rise apartment and one child who plays in your office suite.)

Dream.

HIS **OTHER** LOVE

I hope you will choose not to marry and not to even date someone who is not a Christian or who is not totally living for God. My list, written in November of 1986, is faded and tattered. But I still treasure it and keep it with our family photos. Under this category of His Other Love, my list says three things:

1 Being a Christian isn't enough. He must have insight. He must be growing and willing to try to grow.

2 Spiritual leader—He has to be one who will lead me and others. He must lead me in that he prays first and he encourages devotions for us. He must lead others in that he is involved in service (Sunday school, ministering to friends, being an example, etc.).

3 Similar viewpoints—He must take stands like I do for what I do. He must have the same sort of background. (I think I would like it if he was saved early—like me!)

For me, it was a given that he was going to be a Christian. I wanted to define that a little more with some specific things. I often wrote of this in my journal.

11-25-87 . . . I have no doubt . . . the only reason for marriage is because two can serve God more effectively together than apart. A frightening standard . . . one I can see deceiving myself out of. Few find this relationship. Few need it.

It was so important to me that my husband be a man who was really "going for God." I hope that you want that too. It will save you a lot of heartache in years to come.

Let me tell you why the standard of dating someone who says he is a "Christian" is not enough. I know a woman named Mary. Everywhere I went for years I heard about her. Then I finally met her when she spoke at an event I attended. I could see right away why she was always brought up in conversation. She was blonde, beautiful, and oozed with a contagious enthusiasm. Her speaking style made me envious because she had the skill to make us laugh and cry as she wanted. She talked a lot about her marriage. In college, her husband was a handsome, popular student who had it bad for her. He told her he was a Christian, but she couldn't see a whole lot of "fruit" to back it up. Still, he intrigued and attracted her. Eventually they got married.

Today, he easily confesses that he told her he was a Christian to get her to date him and mostly to get her to sleep with him. Their marriage is filled with pain as he rejects God, desires more to fulfill his own selfish wishes than to love and nurture her, and even suggested they abort their fourth child because it was an inconvenience to him. Though she has a vibrant testimony and is a great encouragement to many, she wishes desperately she had listened to "the little voice inside" of her (probably the Holy Spirit) that told her he "was just saying" he was a Christian.

ISN'T A RELATIONSHIP WITH A NON-CHRISTIAN GUY

A GREAT CHANCE TO WITNESS TO HIM?

Yes, it is.

One of my best friends from high school, Bethany Langham, was a hot item in our dating years. She was smart and outgoing, she had the most beautiful skin and the perkiest nose, and her eyes sparkled when she talked. She drove the guys bananas! I once casually introduced her to a friend of mine named Doug who was not a Christian. Doug desperately wanted to date her and aggressively pursued her. Doug was handsome, fun, and equally pursued by a great number of girls, but Bethany's line had been drawn. Each night that he called to again beg her for a date, she was blunt about it, "Doug, I think you're a great guy, but I need to tell you that I cannot date someone who does not believe what I believe about God." This turned into long inquiries from him about God. Bethany still believes those were his ploys to get her to stay on the phone with him, but she took it as a chance to read him Scripture, pray over him, and blow his mind with the truth of God. But Bethany never, never dated Doug . . . not once. She had her vision for the man she would marry, and it included a godly leader who would challenge, stimulate, and protect her spiritually for the rest of her life. And she got it when she found Jeff Whitcomb, a great big strapping, godly man who all but worships her. I wonder if she would have gotten what she wanted if she hadn't stuck to her dream in every dating opportunity.

PURITY DREAMS OF ITS FUTURE

DANNAH: *What quality most attracted you to your fiancé, Ana? What captured your heart?*

BRETT: Ana really captured my heart because she has such a ferocious love for God. It just pours out of her. I've never met anyone so passionate about knowing God and about making Him known to others. She's not a naturally outgoing person, but in high school she would be so bold about sharing her faith in the classroom, in the dining hall, everywhere she could. I remember one day after we started our relationship where she was just crying and crying because a girl she barely knew had died without knowing the Lord. She takes God's Word and the gospel so seriously. And she's a doer! If she knows God wants her to do something, she does it—even if it hurts and even when her feelings tell her to do otherwise. Most importantly, she's not afraid to challenge me and come alongside me to help me grow. She points me back to God and doesn't let me make excuses for being a lazy follower of Christ. I knew I had to marry her when I saw that she loved Jesus more than she loved me and when I realized that just being with her made me love Him more too. That's what I was looking for and what every Christian guy should be looking for. I pray that each girl reading this book will capture a godly man's heart someday, not because they are trying to get a husband, but because they are madly in love with Jesus.

Be safe. Set a high, high standard in this area. I know that some of you are not.

What does God say? Second Corinthians 6:14 says, "Do not be yoked together with unbelievers." That makes it clear that it's not a good idea to date someone who does not know God and His Son, since dating really is the first step toward marriage. You should not step in that direction with anyone unless he shares your faith. You run the risk of falling in love with someone you simply cannot have. Let me ask you something: Do you want to be intellectually and spiritually superior to the man you fall in love with, or do you want to be challenged and stimulated by him forever and ever? That is entirely your choice.

I am happy to say that eventually God did bring a man into my life who was everything I dreamed of in that list. It was really neat to write, "You are everything" across the list and present it to him one day.

One day you will probably find the special one God has created just for you. Until then, pray for him.

I read in an old issue of *Focus on the Family* about Dolores Cummins of Lindale, Texas, who prayed for her husband before she ever met him. She wrote, "The air was cold that December night. Church bells reminded us to pray for boys trapped in the Battle of the Bulge. I was 15, but I remember hearing a voice saying, 'Your future husband is in that battle—pray!' A year later, I met my

Robert. We started dating, and later we married. To my amazement, he related his experience of lying facedown in a beet field during that battle. The Germans bayoneted nearly all of his fellow soldiers, but they simply stepped over him, sparing his life." I have no doubt that God used her prayers to protect him.

Take a moment right now to start the habit of praying for your future husband. Pray that God would protect him in the physical battles that he faces, but especially the spiritual battles. Pray that God would protect his mind, his body, and his soul until the day that you find him.

Go ahead. Take a moment right now to pray for him.

If the story God writes with your love life is anything like mine, finding him (or waiting for God to bring him to you) will be hard, but not nearly as hard as what follows. It was after I found my husband-to-be that the rest of the secrets became so difficult to execute. But they are worth knowing, because not only did they keep me living a lifestyle of purity, but they also kept him really desiring to pursue me.

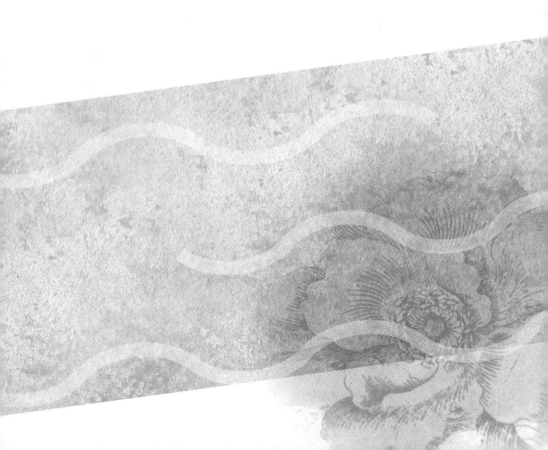

SECRET

3

purity is
governed

by its
value

PART A

CELEBRATION STORY

Agathe Demers on Trusting God

I said yes to Samuel's request to court me by asking him to pie me in front of both of our youth groups! I smiled through the whipped cream and thought, "Finally!"

The journey to that moment required me to wait. A lot. Samuel and I had met upon several occasions in our early college years and eventually became friends. We even exchanged letters for a while. About two years after we stopped corresponding, our paths crossed again. At his initiative we resumed writing to each other. I was afraid to have my heart broken for a second time. The following year we got to know each other quite well, but I was still waiting. It was a struggle at times but I decided to give God control and trust Him. I found out later that Samuel wanted us to not only be good friends but best friends before he asked to court me. The day came when I received a letter from him asking to court me. If my answer was yes, I was to ask him to pie me at the summit of our hike with our youth groups!

I'm so glad I didn't marry the first guy I had a crush on at age seventeen. Because I decided to wait on the Lord, God kept me for my beloved. Samuel is the first and only guy I ever went out with. Praise God for him! We both learned to trust God and serve Him before we were together; we both married our best friend and are now still serving God together. To Him be the glory.

Agathe Demers, Quebec, Canada

purity is governed by its value

Part A: Discovering Your Value in God's Eyes

The king is enthralled by your beauty; honor him,
for he is your lord.... All glorious is the princess within
[her chamber]; her gown is interwoven with gold. In embroidered
garments she is led to the king. (Psalm 45:11, 13–14)

The pile of textbooks and syllabi on my desk looked like Mount Everest, so I'd made the choice to be a responsible college student on this Saturday evening. That was three hours ago, and I'd decided I didn't realize how long Saturday night could get. I sat alone in a massive dorm that was normally full of a couple hundred chattering college girls. Trying to concentrate on my Organizational Communication paper only made the silence more deafening. I needed a friend.

I tried Kimberly. Her roommate answered. "Sorry, Dannah," she said, seeming to know how I felt. "She's out with Jake tonight. I think she took a late pass, so she probably won't be back until after midnight."

My fingers ran through the college phone book. Someone I knew had to be around. I stopped at the Gs.

"Bob Gresh!" I exclaimed. "He'll be around."

It was the running joke that he and his gang could never make up their minds quite what to do. They spent so much time talking about it, they almost never got around to doing anything before it was too late.

I dialed Bob's number in hopes that it was his room they'd decided to deliberate in tonight.

"Hey, what's shakin'?" answered the crazy, familiar voice.

"Hi, Bob! It's me, Dannah," I said. "I'm dateless, friendless, and bored. I need a friend to talk to, and friends are a little scarce around here on a Saturday night."

I'd met Bob nine months previously in Mrs. Harner's Advanced Composition class. He was a comfortable friend. I liked him because he was the class clown, but being in his writing group allowed me a peek into his serious nature. He wasn't just funny and outgoing. His writing told me that he was full of character and conviction. He had vision and was driven to see it through. He was emotional and tenderhearted. He had an uncompromised passion for God. I really respected him.

"When are you going to admit that you are going to marry me?" he asked.

"You are always saying that, silly." I laughed. He was, too, but neither of us thought it meant anything. He was always saying something that meant nothing to get a good laugh.

"I'll be right over," he said.

"What?" I responded.

"We're going on a date," he informed me.

An hour later we were sitting on a park bench, eating the very last of our Crazy Bread and sharing a Frosty. We laughed about Advanced Composition. We showed each other pictures of our families. He acted funny. I laughed at him. We talked about our dreams.

"You're a cheap date," he said, throwing away our trash, as if the conversation was getting a little too deep for him. "I don't mean that in a bad sense, just that you're easily contented."

"This is *not* a date," I said adamantly, smiling at his sudden discomfort at the thought that he may have offended me.

He comfortably reached over and kissed me. It was warm and wonderful, but very unfamiliar.

"*Now* do you think this is a date, Dannah Barker?" he asked as he gazed intently into my eyes.

————————◆◆◆————————

I wish you were here with me right now. I would pamper you nearly to death. I would grab some of my favorite hand lotion—probably pear or peach scented—and I would give you a wonderful hand massage all the way up to your elbows. Then I would take you into my dining room where I would have the table covered in silk and lace. Dainty, valuable teacups would be waiting for us with your favorite steaming tea at the perfect temperature. I would have Godiva biscuits lying in a crystal bowl near your table setting. Close your eyes and go there with me.

Rub your own hands and relax.

Hear the relaxing music in the background.

Imagine the beautiful teacup as you lift it to your lips.

Crunch into that delicious biscuit, smothered in just the right amount of chocolate. Mmmm-mm! This is excellent. I feel pampered. Do you?

Oh, wake up! All I really gave you was a lousy bag of dead leaves in some hot water. That's it! (OK, the Godiva was a bit costly.) But it was not what I gave to you that made you feel special. It was *how* I gave it. The lace and silk and fine china cups gave value to the actual gift. How I presented everything was what made you feel valued.

You see, I could have walked down the hall outside my office to a cold steel machine

Styrofoam Cup, Ceramic Mug, or Priceless Teacup?

TAKE THIS QUICK TEST

Decide in each category whether you are a Styrofoam cup, a ceramic mug, or a priceless teacup. Fill in the box with the appropriate letter. (S=Styrofoam, C=Ceramic, T=Teacup)

- ☐ In the way I dress
- ☐ In the movies I watch
- ☐ In the television shows I watch
- ☐ In the texts I send
- ☐ In the material I view on the Internet
- ☐ In the photos I post on Facebook
- ☐ In the way I talk to girls about guys
- ☐ In the kind of songs I download to my iPod
- ☐ In the places I am willing to go on dates
- ☐ In the things I am willing to do on dates
- ☐ In the things I talk about on dates
- ☐ In the comments I respond to on Facebook
- ☐ In the length of time it takes me to give a guy my heart
- ☐ In the way I treat friends when a dating opportunity pops up
- ☐ In the way I spend time with God specifically talking to Him about guys

HOW DID YOU DO? HOLD THAT THOUGHT. WE'LL COME BACK TO IT.

and, after plunking a few coins into it, brought you a Styrofoam cup full of tea leaves and hot water. There would be no great memories there. I gave you something "trashable."

I could have driven you to the local coffee shop and ordered us a ceramic mug of hot tea and maybe a bagel or something to go with it. That would be OK, but if the mug broke or we never got to go there again, no big deal. The mug wasn't treasured and valued in the highest sense.

But pull in the fine china and silk and lace and Godiva treats and we have a memory that we want to keep around. You and I would both be crushed if one of those precious cups broke. They are treasured possessions to us.

Let me ask you something. In your dating relationships, are you a "trashable" Styrofoam cup, an everyday ceramic mug that is easily replaceable, or a valuable, priceless teacup? It's all in the presentation.

I've heard the saying "Every great love story ends in tragedy" many times lately. Of course, you can quickly point to the very dead Romeo and Juliet as a prime example of this statement. But I'm a hopeless romantic and I don't want to believe that, so I took time to line up some proof that not all great love stories end in tragedy. I found some that don't!

Little Women is really three great love stories that end happily. (Even the story of Jo and Laurie ends happily since they don't do anything they regret.) You can read the classic version by Louisa May Alcott and get the full picture of the great story, or you can rent the video film version starring Winona Ryder for a faster but just as heart-stirring look at the characters' love stories.

In *Pride and Prejudice*, sparks fly when the ever-so-dashing Mr. Darcy meets Miss idealistic-and-independent Elizabeth Bennett. A happily-ever-after that's definitely worth reading. You can catch the American version of the movie if you're short on time, or you can cozy in for the BBC miniseries if you have six hours to spare. Make sure you bring lots of popcorn.

Passion and Purity is a fabulous book detailing the love story of Jim and Elisabeth Elliot. It was also my "handbook" to sexual purity through my college years. Be sure to find a copy of this one.

What I have concluded, as I have read these stories and others, is that great love stories do not have to end in tragedy. However, *a flame of pain fuels every great love story*. The pain comes in one of two packages.

THE **CRASH** AND **BURN**

Your first choice is to have a relationship that is an easy road of blissful moments. The problem is that the relationship could potentially end in a fuel fire of pain. These love stories are written by women who are Styrofoam cups and, sometimes, ceramic mugs. Romeo and Juliet are a great example of this. Juliet wears her heart on her sleeve and throws every caution to the wind to be with Romeo. She defies her parents, sneaks around to be with him, and makes easy, heart-defining choices to have secret moments of bliss with Romeo. In the end, they commit suicide because their relationship is opposed. I do like the story, but I sure would not want it to be *my* great love story. Where's the sunset? Where's the happily-ever-after? (Where's their pulse?)

The girls I have met who choose to make easy, heart-defining choices seem to have no sense of self-value. They are trying desperately to get some kind of guy to desire them at about any cost. Unfortunately, these are often the girls who get trashed at the end of the relationship because they didn't convey any sense of self-value to the guy. I hope you will not choose the crash and burn.

THE **PURE**, SLOW BURN

You can have the sunset love story in your life, but it will mean that you choose the pain that comes in package number two—the pure, slow burn. The pain here is caused by your own self-control, which really feels much like self-denial. As you guard your heart and your body, you can expect to experience some pain. It is far easier, short-term, to be the girl who throws caution to the wind and lets her heart and body

There's Nothing Brief About A Hookup

Today's hookup culture believes it has found a recipe for removing the inconvenience of emotion from sex: friends with benefits. Scientifically, though, that's impossible. We know that thanks to what neuroscientists have learned about a walnut-sized mass in the brain called the deep limbic system. Holding hands, embracing, a gentle massage, and, most powerfully, the act of sexual intercourse work together to create a cocktail of chemicals that records such experiences deep into the emotional center of your brain. It's why we remember sexual experiences and images so clearly. Medical doctors say that these chemicals create a strong bond between sexual partners, almost like glue. The apostle Paul wrote in the New Testament, "Do you know that he who unites himself with a prostitute is one with her in body? For it is said, 'The two will become one flesh.'" Christian author Lauren Winner translates those verses this way: "Don't you know that when you sleep with someone your body makes a promise whether you do or not?" The bottom line is that you get "addicted" and "bonded" to the people you have sex with, even if they are "just friends."

Dannah wrote more about this for CNN's Belief Blog. Read about it by googling "There's nothing brief about a hookup."

become tangled into the moment. *But* if your great love story is fueled by the pain that is caused by wise, head-defined choices in the beginning, it may come with a blissful, happily-ever-after ending. If the relationship does end? You will have no regrets because you have not given your heart or your body away. (And there are still lots of nice clean pages upon which to keep writing your story. One broken relationship is not the end!)

Sense and Sensibility is a great portrait of this kind of love story, but what is so masterful about this classic is that it is laced also with a tragic love story. Elinor is the older sister who falls madly in love with Edward, who is handsome, wealthy, and good-hearted. Throughout her relationship, she is governed by the strictest of choices. She does not allow her heart to be seen. Unfortunately, prior to meeting her, Edward was secretly engaged to another. Being an honorable man, he knows he must not shame the young woman who no longer owns his heart. (I know that sounds ridiculous, but it was written in a different day and age. Stick with me!) Elinor is careful to allow him to remain honorable by not manipulating his heart but by standing free and proud on her own.

Her sister Marianne, on the other hand, falls for Willoughby and lets everyone know it as they race off in his carriage day after day and as she sends him a ridiculous number of unanswered notes. In a great twist, Willoughby marries another for her wealth and leaves Marianne crying at her loss of love, not to mention her loss of integrity.

Meanwhile Elinor takes a call from Edward, who she thinks is married but who has been honorably freed from his commitment. He comes to ask on bended knee for her hand in marriage. A wedding carriage, fresh flower petals, and white horses escort them into the happily-ever-after.

I love Psalm 45. It was written as a wedding song and was probably sung at many Jewish weddings in the days of King David. It's also a wonderful figurative example of what God sees when He looks at you and me . . . the bride of Christ. He

CLICK HERE:

Experience This
Book LIVE!

Like what you're reading? You'll love it even more live and interactive at one of my Pure Freedom events. These are not your typical youth events. You'll figure that out just about the time a girl gets selected from the audience to hit the runway in our fashion show. We have events for teens and their moms and we also have one for your lil' sister and your mom called Secret Keeper Girl. Check 'em out! For current events scheduled or available to bring to your church, visit our website at www.purefreedom.org.

looks upon you and sees a princess. You are a princess. A princess enjoys the great benefits of being waited upon and being adorned with rich tapestry. In my mind, she is calm and contented with where she is today because she knows she is the princess and will someday be married to a marvelous prince.

OK, I know sometimes you may feel more like a frog than a princess, but those are just feelings and they will go away. When I was in high school, I never looked in a mirror. I put my makeup on without looking. (How many silly smudges there must have been!) I felt pretty froglike.

Sometime in my college years, I decided that God had done a pretty good job with me, and it became much easier to be governed by my value because I had begun to feel it. It wasn't just about how I looked, but I had begun to accept how I looked as a part of who and what God valued. It *was* about how I was saturating myself with God's truth. As I began to be filled with His presence, I began to feel the value He placed on me.

The point is this. God says you are a princess. He is *enthralled* by your beauty. Do you believe that? Do you trust the God who made you to be a better judge of your value than the way hormonal days, bad friends, and a crazy schedule can sometimes make you *feel*?

You are a princess. Your behavior and the choices you make must be governed by that value if you are aiming for the sunset ending in your love story. You must present yourself as you would priceless china.

What choices will you make to build a great love story? Will they be choices governed by your heart and your feelings, which can lead to tremendous heartbreak and humiliation? Will you present yourself like "trashable" Styrofoam or an everyday ceramic mug? Or will you make choices governed by your head and the knowledge that you are valued as a princess in God's eyes? Will you be highly valued like a precious piece of china?

Sometimes making choices based on your value may hurt a great deal at first, but they offer you the chance of a great happily-ever-after and will always result in *no regrets*.

WRITE YOUR STORY. Which are you headed for in your life? The crash and burn? The pure, slow burn? Grab your journal and begin with "Based on my own value evaluation, I am headed for the crash and burn/pure, slow burn. Here is why and/or here is what I need to change . . .

SECRET

3

purity is governed

by its value

PART B

Samara Strauss Cone on Staying "Public and Vertical"

After rededicating my life to Christ, I committed myself to remain pure until marriage and sought guidance from any Christian resource I could get my hands on. I recognized that *And the Bride Wore White* was written to a younger audience, but the title appealed to my heart, so I bought it. The most important concept I will always remember is to "stay public and stay vertical"! It seems like such a simple concept, but if I had heard those words when I was younger and guarded them in my heart, I would have saved myself from a lot of heartache! I finally had to lay my desires at God's altar and trust that He knew my heart better than anyone. Two days after I made that commitment, God delivered my prince to me, and he happens to be my prayer partner's older brother! I am happy to say that I am now married to my "Boaz."

Samara Strauss Cone, Florida

purity is governed by its value

Part B: Demonstrating Your Value in the Eyes of Others

*Do you not know that your body is a temple of the Holy Spirit,
who is in you, whom you have received from God?
You are not your own. (1 Corinthians 6:19)*

T his chapter is for the brave and daring. It's about respecting the great weakness God has created in guys. They are made to physically yearn for our bodies. That's not to say that you might not experience some of the same yearning for their bodies, but it is usually far more consuming for men. A University of Chicago sex study said that 54 percent of men thought about sex daily—a number that caused humorist Dave Barry to conclude, "The other 46 percent of the men are lying. Because it's a known scientific fact that all men think about sex a minimum of all the time."[1] (Ha!)

I've seen many studies about this and they vary some, but all agree with one thing. Guys think about sex a lot.

In his bestselling book *I Kissed Dating Goodbye*, Joshua Harris said that his pastor had once asked his youth group to answer the question

"How far have you gone?" They did so using a number scale. After the meeting, Joshua overheard some of the guys bragging about how "high" they had "scored" and with whom in the youth group they had reached a certain number.[2] Yikes!

Sadly, since I originally wrote *And the Bride Wore White*, the mentality of the feminist movement has created what I believe is an unnatural sexual pursuit initiated by girls. (Boy, is that going to be a controversial sentence.) Gloria Steinem, a strong leader in the feminist movement, once said, "A liberated woman is one who has sex before marriage, and a job afterward."[3] Not many Christian girls would say, "Go, Gloria! That's right," but my research with Nancy Leigh DeMoss in writing *Lies Young Women Believe* leads me to conclude that many Christian teens are living as if they believe that statement, even if they would never admit it. So, now we have girls pursuing guys…sexually! I receive frantic letters from moms of teen sons asking what can be done to protect her son from aggressive girls. I get letters from young adult men about how to protect themselves from "cougars." It's out of control!

I am not trying to paint a really ugly picture here, but sometimes young women are terribly naive or they deny the overtly sexual desires that God built into guys. And are using everything in their power of pursue them sexually. Sometimes a girl's actions, clothes, and dating choices are perfectly explosive fuels that may cause a relationship to burst into the flames of a tragic ending. That was not the kind of love story I wanted to write with my life. I hope it is not what you will write with yours.

Since you are a princess, you need to be sure to conduct yourself as one! Here are three areas in which I see girls forgetting to present themselves as valuable, priceless princesses.

THE **ROYAL** WARDROBE

Belly rings. Miniskirts. Short shorts. Low-cut shirts. The fashion world today screams sex. However, clothes don't affect girls and women in the same way as men. That is, we are less prone to be sexually attracted to a guy who is dressing sexually. (Maybe because they don't dress sexually very often, and we're less programmed by it.) Due to our lack of being overstimulated by male immodesty, we continue to wear the latest trends unaware of how it affects a guy. If you are like me, it's a bit hard to get perspective on this since the fashion trends stare us down every single day. So let's grab some perspective by looking at another day and age.

Little Women was written when the fashion was to push a young woman's bust line up to her neckline. (This trend is coming back with the advent of push-up bras created to increase a girl's cup by two sizes. And, tragically, padded bras are being sold for little girls as young as ten! But back to the past.) In the book, beautiful (and normally modest) Meg March went to Annie Moffat's big party. The other girls attending convinced her to let them dress her, complete with a corset and low-cut neckline.

Meg blushed at herself when she looked in the mirror and determined not to let the way she was dressed affect the person she was, *but it did very much affect her.*

Later, Meg admitted the way she was dressed had made her behave badly.

In the movie version of *Little Women,* Meg's mother put it all in perspective, telling Meg, "If you feel your value lies in being merely decorative, I fear you will find yourself one day believing that is *all* you really are."

On your dates and in your everyday life, do you want to be merely decorative, a trait that will someday wear away?

Might I suggest a litmus test for your wardrobe? When you put an outfit on, ask yourself, "Do I feel sexy?" I'm not talking about feeling good or attractive. I am talking about feeling *seductive.* You know what I mean! If you don't know, then you are probably OK. But if you do know, then you probably have a few things in your wardrobe that need to go. If you feel seductive, you probably are, and that can be very dangerous on a date. It will change the way that you behave and the way your date expects you to behave. Be careful in choosing your royal wardrobe.

I FEEL SO STRONGLY ABOUT THE ISSUE OF MODESTY THAT I'VE WRITTEN AN ENTIRE BOOK ON THE SUBJECT. It explores the science of our eyes and guys' minds. I think it'll open up a whole new way of thinking for you. Grab a copy from your favorite local Christian bookstore or from your favorite place to buy books on the Web. There's also a 35-Day devotional book to go along with it.

THE **PRINCESS'S KINGDOM**

So, you're dressed and ready to go. Where should you go? A princess should always stay within the confines of her own kingdom where she is safely guarded under the watchful eye of her public.

I have a friend named Mark who, when he was dating, knew his weakness was to be consumed with his physical desire. Even in his early twenties, he wanted his dating relationships to be governed by some strict principles. So, when Hannah caught his eye, he asked her father for the right to "court" her. They spent "dates" sitting on the sofa in her parents' living room under watchful and loving eyes. They kissed for the first time at the altar of the Lord Jesus Christ as they exchanged vows to love each other for the rest of their lives. Wow! Doesn't that sound tough?

As I have conducted purity retreats, the girls tell me two things about *where* they will go on dates. First, they tell me that nothing good ever happens when they are alone with guys. Their conclusion is always this: if you are truly serious about guarding your innocence and living a lifestyle of purity, you won't go to an apartment, a house, or anywhere where you are truly alone . . . ever. So, how serious are you? Are you serious enough to stay public with your relationship?

Some of the most memorable dates I had with the man who is now my husband were in a laundry facility.

> *1-20-87 . . . We did our laundry together tonight!*
> *10-24-87 . . . A special day with my man. I will remember . . . laughing in the laundry-mat!*

Someplace as ordinary as a laundry facility can be a place for romance to bud. Anyway, the fact is that we could be monitored by "our public," but we were in our own little world as the washers and dryers dulled the sound of others around us. If you want to spend time getting to know a guy, pick a place where your public can watch you while you talk.

The second thing that girls who attend my retreats tell me is that nothing good ever happens in a horizontal position. Even if other friends are around and they're lounging on a beanbag together, they agree that lying down is a bad line to cross. Lying down is very symbolic of letting your guard down. Don't do it. Stay vertical!

A princess should stay where her public can see her and she should stay vertical.

THE **CONDUCT** OF THE **PRINCESS**

Now you've probably got an idea of whom you will be with, how you will dress, and where you will or won't go. Now, how will you act?

In my very first love relationship at the age of fifteen, I did what I see far too many of my favorite girls doing . . . I wore my heart on my sleeve and left it there for the taking. I later wrote:

> *11-7-86 . . . "Be careful of your thoughts, they may break into actions." "Love will always endure if you keep it pure." Those are two sayings I've heard in the past two days that were real meaningful to me. It's so easy to fall into bad situations if you don't build up a very straightforward plan of defense. Believe me. I know.*

Wearing your heart on your sleeve and not being cautious with your actions is not a good idea. It sets you up for great hurt, and, to be honest, guys are not nearly as likely to desperately yearn for you when you are so easily caught! Guys are competitive and have an insatiable need to get what they think they have to earn.

Some of you don't leave much to be earned when you post photos and comments on Facebook. It's one thing to legalistically conform to modesty with your clothes and the places you go, but your conduct betrays a lack of inner modesty.

Kelsey is a high school student who has a reputation as a girl who will do anything with a guy. I'm not sure she has done that much with guys. I think maybe she's gone too far with one, but she's certainly not…well, what everyone calls her but I can't get myself to type. The thing is: on Facebook she invites guys to go places with her that they have no business going. She recently posted a picture of herself on a bed in a skimpy cami and underwear. What was she thinking? I don't know, but it's par for the course with her. But even less overt pictures can be sexual. It's popular to post pictures of just your body, with no head. (What do you want people to look at?) It's popular to tilt your head to the side with a knowing glance that I call the "porn look." (What do you want guys to think about?) It's not OK.

Another popular craze is sexting— sending flirtatious, nude, or seminude pictures of yourself by means of a text message. Because of our unlimited access to immediate communication, it's easy to click "send" without a second thought. But that's what makes it so dangerous. Not only do you run the risk of ruining your reputation if those pictures get around (and they will likely get around), but there's even a chance you could get charged with distributing child pornography. Beyond the potential legal ramifications, sexting leaves nothing to be earned. What guy needs to pursue you romantically when

AUTHOR **BRETT HARRIS** on modesty

DANNAH: *If the girls reading this book were here right now, what would you say to them about how they dress? About how they act?*

BRETT: If I could talk directly to each of the girls reading this book, I'd ask their permission to serve as their big brother for a few minutes. Then I would try to give them a glimpse of how much it pleases the Lord and impresses a godly man when they work hard to dress and act with modesty. The best example of this in my own life is my fiancé and best friend, Ana. When I first started getting to know her, one of the things that really stood out to me is how her clothes and her entire spirit protected me from focusing more on her body than I did on her heart, soul, and mind. And as my dad always said, "What you attract them with, you attract them to." I fell in love with Ana, in part, because of the way she dressed attractively and modestly out of a heart to please God—and I'm not the only guy who feels this way about modesty. According to *The Modesty Survey*, which my brother Alex and I conducted in 2007, over 95 percent of Christian guys surveyed said they notice whether a girl dresses modestly or not, that modesty is an important quality for their future wife to have, and that girls can dress attractively without being immodest. I'd encourage each girl reading this book to go and check out the entire survey. Hundreds of Christian girls contributed questions and over 1,600 Christian guys submitted answers. The survey results don't define modesty, but they can help girls understand how a guy's mind works and how much modesty matters.

Visit the Modesty Survey: www. therebelution.com/modestysurvey he can see all he wants right on his phone? It's not OK. There is much to be learned in the art of inner modesty.

Sometimes it's not photos or poses but what we talk about that betrays a lack of inner modesty. Jill is a freshman in college who is dating an older guy named Jonathan. She has worn her heart all over her sleeve in this relationship. She has told him (and he has told her) that they will be married someday. They've talked of family, dreams, careers, homes, and everything they possibly can. Because they believe they will end up married, they have had a really hard time keeping the relationship pure. I think they just might make it because I see how much they love the Lord and how very much they love each other. But right now, Jonathan is barely interested in pursuing her, and they are taking a "break" from the relationship. He's more interested in his band, his friends, and his future. Why shouldn't he be? He already has her right where he wants her. She is heartbroken and finds it difficult to wake up in the morning.

She is experiencing some of the pain that comes because she made choices characteristic of the "crash and burn" in the area of her conduct. She is as committed to him as if she were married to him and finds herself unsatisfied. In having everything she wanted in the relationship very quickly, she found herself in a period where she has nothing of the relationship. She forgot that she was single. She forgot that she belongs to herself and God during this "season" of her life.

Joshua Harris said, "God gives us singleness—a season of our lives unmatched in its boundless opportunities for growth, learning, and service—and we view it as a chance to get bogged down in finding and keeping boyfriends and girlfriends. But we don't find real beauty of singleness in pursuing romance with as many different people as we want. We find the real beauty in using our freedom to serve God with abandon."[4]

My friend, carefully analyzing the royal wardrobe and staying in the eyes of the public are the easiest things to govern because they are very definable. Determining to remain single and modest in your mind, heart, and reputation until there is a ring on your finger is a much harder element to govern. It requires you to bridle your heart for a time, but I can promise that in the waiting you will find a healthy, growing pain as opposed to the destructive pain of giving your heart away too soon and having it shattered.

Take a look at the women in the Bible. The ones with the big headlines are most often those who bridled their hearts to make wise head choices in relationships. Look at Ruth and . . . let's see, what was her sister-in-law's name? Well, the two of them were stuck with their old

> "The relationship that means most in a man's life is governed by far stricter principles than the casual ones."[5]
>
> Elisabeth Elliot,
> *Passion and Purity*

mother-in-law with no hopes of finding love again. The mother-in-law gave them the chance to follow their hearts and leave. Ruth stayed, though her sister-in-law ran for it. Ruth knew staying was the right thing to do, but it didn't necessarily feel good. Guess what? In the end, God created a rich, beautiful love between her and Boaz *and* they became the great-grandparents of the great King David. Because Ruth was governed by her value and didn't wear her heart on her sleeve, she played a vital role in the lineage of David (and Jesus). Wow! (I wonder what ever happened to her sister-in-law . . . what's-her-face?) What a great love story— far better than the one she may have written with her life if she had forgotten her value and allowed her life to be governed by her heart.

WRITE YOUR STORY. OK. Now it's time to work it! I'd like you to do three things with your journal. Take your journal into your clothes closet or sit with it next to your dresser or wardrobe. Look through your clothes and kick out what needs to go.

Now, tell God how good that feels. While you're in there writing, jot down some thoughts on where you can go on a date where you live—places that allow you to stay public!

Finally, talk to God about your heart. Write down the names of people you've given it to and ask God to reclaim it. Trust Him to write a love story beyond your wildest imagination. Determine to be governed by your value, not your heart.

The night that I first "dated" Bob, I knew I needed to be governed by my value. I could tell that he fit my list and I was interested in dating him—for "real," next time. But I had really blown it. *I* had called *him* . . . how desperate does that look? I let him *kiss* me on our first date . . . how easy does that seem? I was determined to begin to make some tough choices that better reflected my value. That might mean fewer blissful moments but had the promise of a happily-ever-after ending loosely attached.

The next time I saw Bob after I realized my poor beginning, I had the list *and* I was ready to let my value in God's eyes govern my behavior. He drove by in his little white sports car, backing up when he saw me. I was walking away from him on the pathway to my dorm.

"Hey, Dannah Barker, come here," he called. My heart jumped and every muscle ached to turn and hop into that car like I had so many times in the past few weeks.

"Why?" I probed.

"Because you adore me," he claimed.

"Oh, do I?" I smiled at him and then turned to keep walking.

"Dannah Barker, come back here," he called as I calmly kept walking toward my destination.

"Chase me!" I challenged and confidently walked into my dorm.

THE LINE

If you truly are "governed by your value," you should never find yourself in a compromising situation. Unfortunately, I know some of you will find yourselves in that position, anyway. Are you prepared to stop things? Let's walk through this together. Look at the "steps to physical intimacy" sidebar.

1 *Draw a firm black line right above the step where you will stop any type of physical contact.* Predetermining where you will stop things will help you when temptations arise. It will set off a mental alarm for you. (Remember, God designed you and me to naturally desire to move to the next step. It is not easy to stop the desire to progress. Be very conservative—oh, what a word—about where you draw this firm black line!)

2 *Now, take time to prayerfully consider . . . would God be pleased to see you doing the particular physical activity directly below that firm black line?* If you have any doubt at all, go back to number one and reconsider your choice. Remember God desires that you do not have even a "hint" of sexual immorality within your life.

3 *Finally, let me suggest the option of drawing a line at a lower level of physical activity before you are engaged.* For example, let's say you drew your firm black line above number five. You have determined that your firm black line will remind you to stop as soon as soft kissing begins to turn into something more passionate. I desire for you to unquestionably not go beyond that line when you are engaged. That can be hard. Your body and your mind are tellin' you that you've almost made it, and temptation can really blindside you. (But, oh, you *have* almost made it. Don't blow it here.) I am not saying you have to, but wouldn't it be neat to save that special intimacy for your engagement! Push yourself. Draw a dotted line at a lower level and determine not to go beyond that line until you are engaged.

What decisions do you need to make in your current dating behavior that will protect you from going too far, too soon? Keep in mind that you must stop before you have any desire to be more physically intimate with someone. For many, that means holding hands is too far.

9 Sexual intercourse

8 "Experimental" nakedness / oral sex

7 Petting while clothed /mutual masturbation (Touching each other naked.)

6 Anything above the waist goes! (That's right. He's up your shirt!)

5 "Hooking up" with your clothes on. (You get the idea. Clothes on, but you're in full-out make-out on top of each other.)

4 A gentle kiss. (Maybe on the cheek or nose. A brush of the lips.)

3 Hands on shoulders and hands on waist. (A definite sign that romance is in the air.)

2 Holding hands. This is a nice sign of attachment. (It says you like each other. Your relationship is growing.)

1 Cuddle sitting . . . shoulder to shoulder. (You're happy to have your space invaded.)

STEPS TO
Physical Intimacy

Be governed by your value. Like a priceless piece of china, the way you present yourself deserves great care. Take the time to carefully draw a firm, uncrossable line, using the suggestions on the opposite page.

Adapted from Greg Johnson and Susie Shellenberger, *What Hollywood Won't Tell You About Sex, Love, and Dating* (Ventura, Calif.: Regal, 1994), 17–18.

SECRET

4

purity

speaks

boldly

Joanna Walker on Saving Her First Kiss

I was on my own at seventeen. Because of my abuse-filled childhood, I had determined in my heart to live life God's way. That included dating. So I sat down and searched the Bible for a list of character traits to look for in a man. There were about 12 items on the list, and as I read over them I realized that this man probably wouldn't even consider me. So I made another list—33 items, titled "Requirements for the Woman Who Marries My Husband." My standards were costly: I spent three and a half years of college dateless and lonely. But I wouldn't budge on my requirements either for a man or for myself.

One day in conversation with one of my coworkers, I told him that I was going to wait until my wedding day for my first kiss. He laughed and said, "Good luck finding a guy to go along with that plan. It certainly won't be me!" It didn't bother me because that was often the reaction I got, and besides, I had already dismissed any possibility of him being the one. But as I watched him over the next several months, I was shocked to realize that one by one God was showing me the character traits on my list . . . in him. As our friendship developed I realized that I was falling in love. I immediately started to pull away because if he still wasn't willing to honor my commitment to have the first kiss be on my wedding day, I knew I couldn't date him. It was then that he asked me to meet him for breakfast the next day. Afterward he knelt in front of me with a ruby ring and asked me to wear it opposite my purity ring. He asked me to court him and expressed his commitment to purity. Two years later he asked me to marry him.

I have never regretted for a moment my choice to walk in purity. And I will never forget my first kiss.

Joanna Walker, Florida

purity
speaks
boldly

Preparing Your Tongue for Dates

*Do not let any unwholesome talk come out of your mouths, but
only what is helpful for building others up according to their needs,
that it may benefit those who listen. (Ephesians 4:29)*

*10-4 . . . It pays to do things the hard way, which is the case more
often than not when you seek the Lord's will. My relationship
with Bob Gresh is more unique and special than it ever has been.
There are not any "I love yous," there are no physical displays of
affection, and yet our relationship runs more deeply now than
when those things were present. It's not easy. There are days I
don't share with him and yet I'm so thankful that the Lord has given us
the wisdom to patiently wait for His timing.*

*11-13 . . . I argued with Bob tonight. No, we didn't fight, but we
enthusiastically debated our views. I never even knew I had it in me.
Debate is somehow stimulating. In fact, if we hadn't been disagreeing,
I'd have been laughing.*

I laid down my journal, having read the slow progression of several months of a relationship I was treasuring. Our hearts, which for a few weeks were so easily read and unguarded in our passion, had reverted to an unspoken determination by our heads to progress slowly . . . painfully slow.

However, there was a sense of an upcoming reward to the pain of waiting. I wasn't afraid in this relationship because I was not entirely vulnerable. I felt no risk of becoming overly physical because that was in no way a part of our relationship. And best of all, there were still some incredible moments ahead of us. I did not realize it, but I was about to experience one of them.

I glanced at the clock and realized it was time to meet Bob at my dorm lobby. He met me, escorted me to his car, and we got in. As we drove away, the conversation picked up where we'd left off the last time we'd been together. We had a pace to our conversation. It was aggressive and determined. We had no awkward pauses as we wondered what to say next. We were on a mission to chisel into each other's minds and were using words as our primary tool.

Suddenly, he stopped the car. I noticed the soft January snowflakes for the first time and felt the hush of a fresh snowfall embrace our car. It was as if time had suddenly stopped.

He reached over and tenderly kissed the tip of my nose, barely brushing my lips as he pulled away.

"*This* is as far as I want any physical contact to go between us," he whispered and then drove on. We were silent for the first time in months. I pondered the unspoken words he had *not* used to charge me with a great task.

I heard him.

He was asking me to keep talking.

I did.

The tongue is a powerful tool. James compares it to the rudder of a great ship. With just this little instrument, you can set your course for a direction toward something great or toward the perils of an iceberg.

Though somewhat of an introvert, I found that keeping my lips loose kept my relationship headed toward greatness. I've seen a trend as I counsel young women in their relationships. Author Robert Wolgemuth spoke of it in his book *She Calls Me Daddy*. He said that young women who have learned the art of conversation are less likely to be caught in compromising physical situations. Why? "First, assuming that boys will nearly always be the aggressors, [you'll] know how to openly express [your] commitments to purity and . . . fears of the consequences of premarital intimate contact. Second, young lovebirds usually choose between talk and the backseat. They don't do both simultaneously."[1]

If you truly desire to live a lifestyle of purity, you'll learn the secret of speaking boldly.

LOAD YOUR LAP WITH TENNIS BALLS

Wolgemuth was taking his young daughters to a friend's home for dinner one evening when a conversation skill came in handy. Similar to pre-date jitters, the girls found themselves nervous about what to say and how to act. He told them to fill their laps with tennis balls before they sat down for dinner and be ready to throw them at their new friends. I am sure the girls' eyes were as wide as tennis balls when their dad announced they'd be throwing balls at the dinner table, but he went on to explain. The tennis balls were really questions, and when their new friends answered, it would be like another tennis ball coming back to them that needed to be caught. Then the girls could decide if it was a good ball that needed to be thrown back or if it was a bad one . . . in which case they would pick up a new question from their lap and toss it out.[2] It's a great concept. Do you have a lapful of tennis balls for your dates?

Here are some questions that could stimulate conversation if you're feeling awkward:

- Do you play sports?

- What kind of car would you like to have? Why?

- Who are your heroes? Why?

- Have you ever been on a missions trip? Where?

- What are your top three memories of your grandparents?

> **"LET'S BE CANDID WITH OURSELVES BEFORE GOD.**
>
> Call a spade a spade or even a muddy shovel. If your passions are aroused, say so—to yourself and to God, not to the object of your passion. Then turn the reins over to God. Bring your will to Him. Will to obey Him; ask for His help. He will not do the obeying for you, but He will help you. Don't ask me how. He knows how. You'll see."[3]
>
> Elisabeth Elliot
> *Passion and Purity*

Another great way to get questions is to go back to your dream list that you should have written in chapter 7. This is your chance to find out if he is worth the ink on that list!

- So, what do you wanna be when you grow up? *(Look for that compatibility in goals and dreams.)*

- What's your mom like? *(A man is often looking for a wife who is similar to her!)*

- Tell me about your church. *(A good nonthreatening look at his commitment to the Lord.)*

- Do you feel close to God? *(He better if you think he's got a good chance of being great for God.)*

WATCH THE FOUL LINES

I'm using this illustration of tennis balls, or conversation balls, as a great way to encourage you to speak boldly. But any great ball game has boundaries, and if the ball moves outside of the boundaries, you foul or you lose control of the ball. You need to watch the foul lines in your communication, as well.

By now you can tell that I was a little old-fashioned in my dating because I was confident that some old-fashioned dating was not only safe for the heart and the body, but it also drives a guy's heart right into a girl's hands. So, in honor of our last chapter . . . you need to set some guidelines about what you will and will not discuss. For me it was rather simple. I had determined two foul lines and one "technical."

FOUL LINE 1

I will not discuss marriage to him until he romantically and lovingly makes the commitment to ask me to marry him.

I wanted the fairy tale and that included a bended knee, so I was determined not to spoil it by stealing the moment too early in any relationship. My husband and I did talk about marriage before we were engaged, but in a general sense and after we'd been dating for a good year and a half. We discussed things like how many children we each dreamed of having one day or what kind of home we hoped to own. They were all very general discussions, and the focus was on his dreams or my dreams, but never *our* dreams.

"NADA 'TIL YADA"

In all the years, this is my favorite comeback line. It came from a teenager who heard me speak from my book for college-aged girls *What Are You Waiting For: The One Thing No One Ever Tells You About Sex.* In it, I trace God's word for sex in the Old Testament: yada! Check it out!

FOUL LINE 2

I will not discuss sex, physical contact, or my physical desires with him.

A few months ago, I took a college-bound friend of mine to St. Louis for the day. She confided that she and her boyfriend struggled physically, so they talked about it . . . in detail. How her body felt. How his responded. What she desired. What he dreamed of. As soon as I got home, I grabbed one of my friends and said, "Did you and your husband ever talk about your desires when you were dating?" "No way," she answered.

"That would have made it far too difficult not to fulfill them and, in fact, would have been way sexier than actually fulfilling them."

At the same time, it's really common to talk about your period or your body in front of guys. It may be normal, but it's not God's best. For example, it's normal for a guy to want to study the Victoria's Secret poster at the mall, but it's not God's best for him. It's normal for a man to think sexually about a woman he's not married to who dresses immodestly and flirts with him, but it's not God's best. It's normal to want to watch a funny television show that's full of sexual jokes, but it's not God's best. Talking about your body in front of guys may be normal, but it also normalizes sexual familiarity and that's a risk to your purity!

Please, oh please, remember the power of your tongue. The brain is the greatest of all sexual organs. When guys are visually stimulated and when you and I are emotionally stimulated, specific chemicals are released within the brain to cause us to desire sexual activity. The one thing that has the potential to stimulate both male and female is conversation. So determine not to talk about your desires, as it will make it very difficult to control them.

RECORDING ARTIST REBECCA ST. JAMES ON THE POWER OF THE TONGUE

DANNAH: *How important is it to talk about your boundaries in relationships?*

REBECCA: Talking about boundaries is incredibly important. My husband and I, before we were married, spoke about boundaries and how we were both committed to purity. He waited as well. We just said, "We're not going to lie on a bed together until after we're married. We're not going to touch each other or take clothes off where a modest bathing suit would cover. We need to be very God-honoring. God is watching us, and how would He feel about what we're doing right now?" These are the kinds of things that we discussed. In Christian community we say, "Do we really need to specify that [we're not going to take clothes off]?" When you love somebody, it's easy to start rationalizing things, so I think talking about boundaries is a really important element.

DANNAH: *In your latest book* What Is He Thinking, *you interviewed a bunch of guys to get their thoughts on girls and dating. What did you discover?*

REBECCA: One was a super encouraging thing: to find out that even if guys encounter a super attractive, beautiful woman, if she doesn't have a personality that they're drawn to and a heart for God, they're really not interested after a date or two. If she's a hot girl who's boring, they're not interested. Hearing them verbalize that it's about more than a pretty face was so encouraging. Because I think our culture fills us with this lie that it's almost entirely about appearance. Like, guys just want a super attractive girl. All of us girls deal with some kind of body image insecurities anyway, so it just adds so much more pressure to dating if we feel like that outer package is just about all guys are looking for. Over and over again, I felt like I was hearing from these guys, "We want to be drawn to the heart and soul of a girl, not just the outer appearance." That was awesome.

This is also confirmed biblically. In the Song of Solomon, the Bible's great love story, the two lovers used passionate, loving words to awaken desires. Talk is intimate. If you are convinced that the relationship you are in is the godly dream that you have written about in your list and you have determined that you are ready to be married, pursue this person with lots of talk. Just take care what you talk about.

AVOIDING A **TECHNICAL OFFENSE**

I will communicate a desire to live a lifestyle of purity.

If you are caught "traveling" in basketball, you lose control of the ball. If you have a "hand ball" in soccer, you lose the ball. Technical offenses cause you to lose control of the game, and you have to work extra hard to regain your offensive position. You end up playing defense. I had determined that I was not going to commit the "technical" of failing to communicate my desire to live a lifestyle of purity. I was going to stay on the offense.

Mostly, this is communicated nonverbally, in the way that you dress, where you will go on a date, and the simple body cues you offer. But there may be occasions when it needs to be communicated more blatantly.

I heard every word Bob Gresh *did not speak* to me that night when he said, "This is as far as I want our relationship to go." He was saying, "This is hard for me. I physically yearn for more, but I need you to hold me accountable to my desire to live a lifestyle of purity." Previously, I had made my own desire for purity known by playfully saying things like, "We kiss too much. I've got brains too, ya know." And, "Do you want to get to know me or my lips?" That put the end to our foolish beginning and got us headed toward something great.

Confessing your wish to be pure does two things: (1) It creates accountability to each other to live up to it, and (2) it sets the standard. Notice that in my confrontation to Bob there was little detail as far as the desires that were awakened.

LOOSE LIP CONTRACT

I will keep my lips loose on a date. I commit to do the following:

I will begin each dating relationship with a "tennis ball" load of questions.

Once I have found someone who meets my dream list, I will date him using these guidelines for conversation . . .

I will not discuss marriage to him until he romantically and lovingly makes the commitment to ask me to marry him.

I will not discuss sex, physical contact, or my desires with him.

I will communicate a desire to live a lifestyle of purity.

_____
Signature

_____
Date

Commit to communicate this nonverbally as you are "governed by your value" and seek to "speak boldly," but if the need or occasion arises, be prepared to draw the line quickly and with little detail about your physical desires.

Controlling the tongue is not easy. Since the tongue is so powerful, I'd like you to review by signing the contract for your lips on page 100!

Keep reading because the next secret proved to be the most crucial one to assure me of a satisfying marriage.

TOP TEN COMEBACK LINES

OK, things have gone too far. He is reaching for the forbidden fruit . . . or maybe you are. It is time to say, "Freeze." What words will you use to do it? I've been collecting these comeback lines since this book came out a few years ago and I love hearing your ideas. Be sure to join my Dannah Gresh Facebook page and send me your ideas! Below I have given you two of the best comeback lines I have heard. You determine what other eight you will add to your list.

10. *Isn't it cool that God is watching us every minute?*

9. *Hey, have I told you that my father dusts me for fingerprints when I get home from a date?*

8. _____

7. _____

6. _____

5. _____

4. _____

3. _____

2. _____

1. _____

WRITE YOUR STORY. It's time to commit. Your lips are very powerful. You need to make a commitment with the loose lips contract, *but only if you intend to stick to it.* If you feel that you have failed in one of these four areas, take your journal out and write about it. Then, commit right here and now by signing the loose lip contract.

SECRET

5

CHAPTER ELEVEN

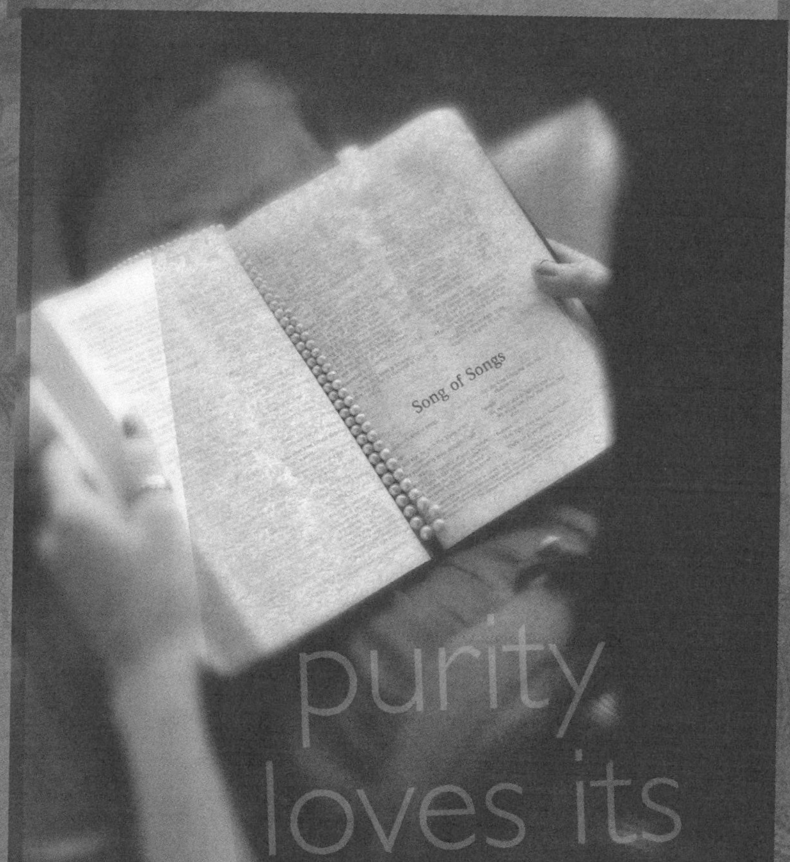
Song of Songs

purity loves its creator at any cost

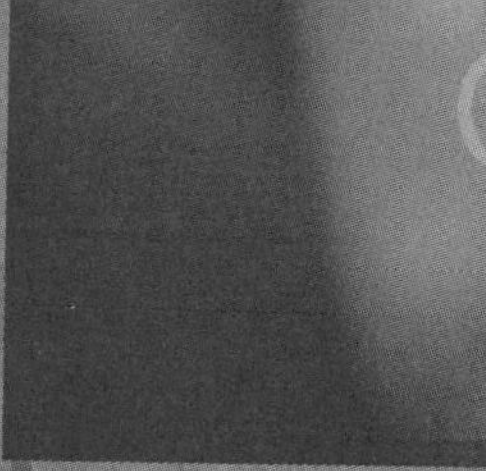

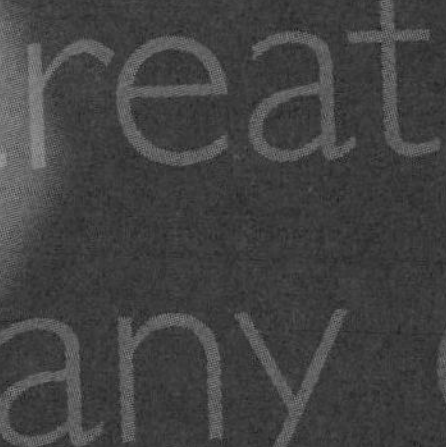

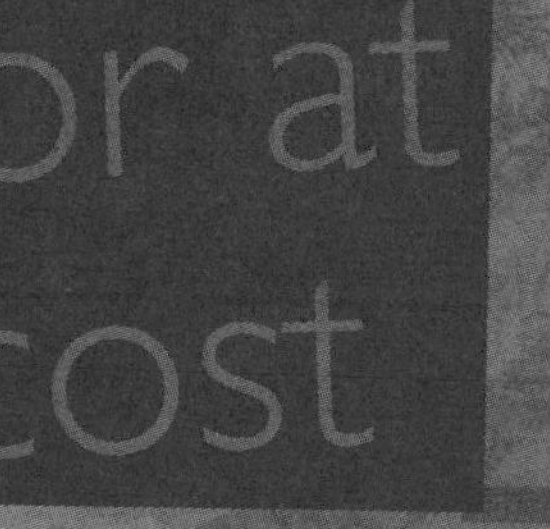
Song of Songs

Katie Myers on Loving Jesus

As I browsed the shelves at a local Christian bookstore, a pretty book with the title *And the Bride Wore White* popped out at me. I quickly dismissed it though. I had just ended a fairly serious relationship, and such a title made me uncomfortable. I continued browsing and met my friend at the front of the store to compare finds. She showed me a few books and then handed me one saying "and I thought this one looked interesting."... It was *And the Bride Wore White*!

I decided to take a closer look and then surprised myself by buying it! I didn't know it then, but I was on the brink of a brand-new life. Looking back I can clearly see how the Spirit was leading me and preparing me to open the door to wholly accepting Jesus into my life. Reading *And the Bride Wore White* helped me to realize that I need to stop searching for fulfillment in romantic flings and that there is a whole lot more to purity than not having sex until marriage. It has given me a new hope for a future that will be in God's will, and a life that is meaningful. The God of the universe **loves** me, and that knowledge allows me to wake each day in obedience, with joy and expectation.

Katie Myers, Pennsylvania

This book conjured up questions in Katie's heart. She contacted me, and we eventually met for coffee to talk. At the meeting, she asked Christ to be her Savior. She's currently training for the mission field!

purity loves its creator at any cost

Pursuing a Love Relationship with Jesus

*The kingdom of heaven is like a merchant looking for fine pearls.
When he found one of great value, he went away and sold
everything he had and bought it. (Matthew 13:45–46)*

I could not imagine my life without Bob Gresh. Life with him was
full and free and adventuresome. He made me feel confident,
capable, and intelligent. His words catapulted me often into
what we had come to call "dreamy numbness."

But this week I had made some bad choices. I had skipped
an important yearbook meeting when Bob had called at the
last minute to take me to Wittenberg Library. Instead of looking up
the Bible verses when the pastor encouraged us to do so in church, I
had opted to keep holding Bob's big, warm hand. And my roommate,
Kimberly Sweet, had given me a kind confrontation about how I was
allowing my friendship with Bob to squeeze out my friendship with
her and just about everyone else. Our last few dates had included

some passionate kissing. My journal had become full of him and not God. After a year and a half of "pure, slow burning," I was beginning to slowly ease my way back into "crash and burn" mode.

So here I was in his apartment, standing awkwardly near the door.

"Come in," he encouraged.

"I can't," I said as a tear slipped down my cheek and my lips began to quiver. He had never seen me cry. He quickly began to move toward me with his arms outstretched.

"No, don't," I softly demanded. "Listen to what I have to say first."

He stopped with the sofa the only object seemingly holding us from each other's arms.

"I treasure our friendship," I began. "I know that you do too. But we have got to be more in each other's spiritual lives than just someone to sit next to in church."

The look in his eyes told me he understood. I was not telling him we could not go on *like this*. I was not suggesting to him that we could change it. I was telling him we could not go on.

Our eyes never lost the intent, direct gaze as tears flooded our faces. Desperately wanting to hold each other, but knowing that might lead to more easy choices, we stood staring into each other's pain. After a long silence, he spoke.

"I know," he whispered, and we continued looking at each other hopelessly. I prayed silently for strength to carry through as my heart felt as if it was physically ripping within me and my body felt as if huge boulders were suddenly pushing me toward the floor.

"Oh, God," I said in my head. "I have never sacrificed something to You that I hold so dear. I don't know if You will give him back to me, but I will trust You to fill this huge void in my heart someday, somehow. Please, let it be him. Please, my dear Jesus."

After nearly a half hour of standing there in the silence of our pain and listening to the clock tick, I turned and quietly opened the door and left. I did not know if the door to this precious relationship would ever be opened again.

I know only one thing that is free, and that is God's loving forgiveness. But that short parable that Jesus told about the merchant and the pearl of great price says that to really pursue God, know God, and love God may require selling all that you have. God asks that we trade in all the fake pearls of our life to buy the real pearl. He says in Luke 14:33 that "any of you who does not give up everything he has cannot be my disciple."

secret #5: purity loves its creator at any cost

In my original Pure Freedom event, I gave the girls who attended a price tag that said "Everything costs something. Some things cost everything." Then we listened to testimonies about the cost of "fake pearls" in our lives.

One girl, Kylie, told how she hated the label of being "innocent" so she started being flirtatious to be more fun. One of her good friends stopped her and said, "I miss innocent Kylie. I liked her better. She was real." Kylie left the retreat knowing she was going to have to set some things straight and it was not going to be easy. In fact, she was expecting it to cost her some friendships.

Mikayla had been running with some girls with bad attitudes in her youth group. They joked around and took lightly the things of God. Right before I conducted a retreat at her church, she began to experience real spiritual revival in her life. Then she and her friends came to the retreat. As she melted into God's arms at the retreat, her friends began to get nervous. They cruelly taunted her and teased her as others watched. Running with the wrong crowd was costing Mikayla something as she began to make right choices.

A young adult woman named Tanisha cried admitting she was grateful that she kept her baby when she got pregnant a few years ago. But it was hard. While her friends were pursuing dreams, available for dates, and living a young adult life, she is living the hard life of a single mom. And the cost is loneliness and hard work.

Ashley talked about being the most popular girl with the guys in high school and college. Then, she talked about having cervical cancer at the age of twenty-six. She knew it was because she'd had so many sexual partners and had acquired HPV. She had to have a full hysterectomy and would never have babies.

TODAY'S PEARLS

We just don't "get" the value of pearls since we live in a culture that creates them. Jesus lived in a culture that knew their true value. Did you know that when He was on earth the only way to find a pearl was to dive into the ocean and find mollusks . . . not one but thousands? In fact, a man had to open up 15,000 mollusks to find just one pearl, and it may or may not have been one of great value. How many did he have to pry open to find that precious pearl of great value? So rare was the valuable pearl that often a man did have to sell all that he had—his land, his livestock, his servants, his home—to have enough to buy just one pearl of great value. I wonder if we're willing to pursue Christ with such passion?

There's always a cost to what we invest in. The costs of "fake pearls" can be great. Giving your body away might someday need to be paid for in the form of pregnancy, AIDS, or some other STDs. Giving your heart away could end in heartbreak and spiritual anemia.

AUTHOR BRETT HARRIS ON LOVING CHRIST

DANNAH: *What has been the biggest blessing of following the Creator at any cost?*

BRETT: The biggest blessing of following the Creator is the Creator. The greatest reward for pursuing a closer relationship with Jesus Christ is Jesus Christ. For example, as I get closer to my fiancé, Ana, I experience many benefits from her. When I'm with her she might make me some really good food or make me laugh harder than I ever have before. When we're apart she might send me a really sweet card or text message. But even with all those wonderful blessings, the best thing about my relationship with Ana is Ana. If something were to happen to her so she was unable to ever make me another meal or write me another card, I would still marry her because I love *her* far more than I love the things she does for me—and it should be the same way with God.

The apostle Paul wrote, "But whatever things were gain to me, those things I have counted as loss for the sake of Christ. More than that, I count all things to be loss in view of the surpassing value of knowing Christ Jesus my Lord . . ." (Philippians 3:7–8 NASB). Paul was willing to lose everything to know Christ because what he really wanted was Christ. Most of us aren't willing to follow Christ at any cost because really, if we're honest, we care more about the benefits of obeying God than we do about God. We come to Jesus on our way to something else we want even more. We try to be godlier so we'll feel better about ourselves or so a certain godly (and cute) member of the opposite sex will notice us. If that's true, we need to repent and ask God to forgive us. We need to cry out to God to change our hearts so we can say with Paul, "Yes, everything else is worthless when compared with the priceless gain of knowing Christ Jesus my Lord" (Philippians 3:8 NLT).

Even seemingly "good" things can be fake pearls if they haven't had time to be cultured into the real thing. My relationship with Bob was like that. So we "sold" it to pursue God's best. The cost was great. During our breakup Bob's journal had many entries like this . . .

My dearest Dannah,

Being without you takes a lot of getting used to. Since this is my journal let me be completely honest. There is a large part of me that doesn't miss you right now; a large part that feels no emotions, no loss. However, there is also a large part of me that feels tremendous loss, almost a loss of hope.... There seems to be no life without you, Dannah. I have come to depend completely upon you. The absence of deep roots of God in my life is an unexplainable mystery. My heart is deceitful and desperately wicked. I am the least and yet there is hope. Sad thing is that I can't envision it anymore. The light has gone out. It is dark.

Love, Bobby

I never saw that journal entry until we were engaged. But I had written several much like it.

9-27–87. . .God is sovereign. Jesus is enough. Those are my spiritual goals. The day I believe in them completely is the day I am ready for a relationship. That day seems so far away. Lord, give me patience.

10-10-87. . . My head knows the path that I must take, but my heart is one tough muscle. Today in chapel Joseph Stowell said, "God will not do by miracle what I am to do by obedience." I sure wish He could do this by miracle. Obeying is very painful.

1-19–88. . . "Thou wilt keep him in perfect peace, whose mind is stayed on thee," Isaiah 26:3 (KJV). Tonight I write only what God is saying to me . . . not out of fear that someone would read what I feel in my heart, but rather because I am afraid to articulate feelings I might have to destroy.

Today, those journal entries are proof of how much our relationship was more important to us than our God and of how we were sacrificing something precious so that our relationship with God could be our most priceless possession.

On December 6 of that year, I attended a Sunday school class taught by Bob. We were still not together, but my heart was healing and becoming stronger in the Lord. In the class, he read Matthew 13:45–46, which says, "The kingdom of heaven is like a merchant looking for fine pearls. When he found one of great value, he went away and sold everything he had and bought it." His journal from the night before outlined his message that day.

The Lord has taught me much in reading His Word tonight.

They can be summed up in five statements:

1. *There is a pearl of great price.*

2. *We are to seek it.*

3. *We are commanded to purchase it.*

4. *It costs us everything.*

5. *It is worth the price.*

*I must come to the point where I stop the payments on the fake pearls
in my life and start making the payment on the real pearl.
God costs everything. He is worth the price.*

Bob had come to realize that if he wasn't willing to relinquish all the fake pearls in his life, he would never fully understand the full blessing of God's goodness.

Giving up each other had been such a portrait of that verse in our lives. I had watched so many of my girlfriends return from Thanksgiving break with huge engagement rings on their fingers. I smiled through my pain and congratulated them. I had many lonely, quiet Friday and Saturday nights. I had to confess my negligence to several friends and ask them to let me back into their lives. Bob and I had several classes together that quarter, and seeing him every day only resurfaced the pain I had worked at alleviating in my prayers.

During that time, my theme was "God is sovereign. Jesus is enough." Until I felt that in my heart, I had determined not to date Bob or anyone else.

WRITE YOUR STORY. What are the fake pearls in your life? Please believe me that the sacrifice of them is worth the cost. What God can give you is so much more valuable. Take a moment right now to write a love letter to God and admit to Him what fake pearls you are clinging to with your lifestyle. Be honest and tell Him that there is a part of you that treasures these fake pearls and you really find it hard to surrender them. But trust Him to replace them with something far better. Now would be a good time to stop and do this.

Eleven days after Bob taught that Sunday school class on the pearl of great price, I went to my mailbox to find an envelope with my name scrawled in his handwriting. In it, he wrote

Matthew 13:45–46

*"The kingdom of heaven is like a merchant looking for fine pearls.
When he found one of great value, he went away and sold everything
he had and bought it."*

He costs everything. He is worth the price.

You cost everything. You're worth the price.

I did not realize it, but he had begun to understand that there would be one relationship between him and a woman, which was a portrait of the condition of his love for God. He was having a hard time waiting, but he was sending me some of his desire that I might wait along with him for God to culture us. We both had a lot of loving to do in our relationship with God before we would be ready to love each other. We continued the long process of waiting.

Months went by, yet we did not feel God's release to be together.

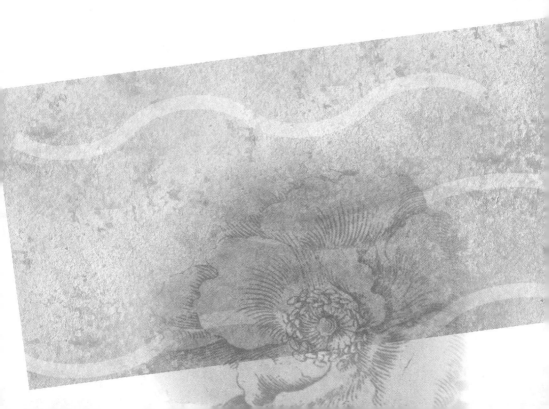

SECRET

6

purity

embraces
wise
guidance

Jen Wilton on Talking to Her Mom

It seemed impossible! My mom and I had never really been close. How could I possibly tell her about my past—about the biggest mistake I had ever made? I was terrified of what her reaction would be. A year and a half had passed since I had seen him. I'd seen Dannah Gresh on television and communicated with her. She helped me through this difficult time. On several occasions, she brought up the idea of talking to my mom about it. After a long inner struggle one night, I forced myself out of my room and up the stairs to my mom's room. I walked in, sat down, and began to tell her about what had happened over a year and a half earlier. I began to cry as I told her what I was still going through and dealing with— all the guilt and shame. She didn't get angry or upset with me; she just calmly sat and listened to what I had to tell her. She told me how she had sat up in her room some nights crying. She had felt so helpless, because she saw me day after day, crying in my room alone, but she had no idea what was wrong with her "little" girl. I was AMAZED at her reaction. I had NO idea she cared so much! And oh the freedom I felt! It was as though something had been lifted off of me! And after all this, my mom and I became a lot closer. Our relationship just seemed to immediately change. I could now talk to her and be open with her about everything because I had nothing left to hide.

Jen Wilton, pictured here with Dannah in Ontario, Canada

Jen—or Jengy, as I call her—wrote that a few years ago when we first revised this book. Since then, she has served in ministry on my Pure Freedom team and is currently in youth ministry in Canada. Be sure to check out her letter at the end of the book!

purity embraces wise guidance

Inviting Your Parents into Your Love Life

*Honor your father and your mother,
so that you may live long in the land the
Lord your God is giving you. (Exodus 20:12)*

L "*Lisa, my mom is going to call me tonight,*" I said as I walked out the door, a load of laundry under one arm.

"Did she tell you that?" asked Lisa, seeing the mischief in my eye.

"No, but she will call," I said with certainty. Lisa was running down the hall minutes later to get me from the laundry room. After a few moments of encouragement across the miles, we hung up and I grabbed my journal.

10-18–87 . . . 1 Thessalonians 3 says that Paul sent Timothy to encourage the afflicted church. Kind of like my mom encouraging her afflicted daughter. I love her so much.

My mom had just endured two days of travel with a wild-eyed freshman to and from Pennsylvania and Ohio. She had stayed for two nights in a guys' apartment where she deemed the highest nutrient value was to be found in the ring of the bathtub rather than any boxed food in the kitchen. She'd done it for me. Because my heart was hurting and it made me feel valued. I went to bed that night feeling so loved.

The next morning after my 9:00 class, I walked with Lisa to the "Po," as we called the Cedarville College Post Office. It was a welcomed treat of the day. Everyone hoped there might be a pink "You have a package waiting" card or a note from a special someone. On this particular day, I recognized the sloppy handwriting indicating that my special someone was my high school brother, Darin. True to reputation, the card itself was humorous but its purpose was to encourage me during this season of waiting. Under his name he had taken time to write, "I bet you are like a proton surrounded by an entire galaxy of electrons with guys just waiting to get their turn to take you out."

It was the boost I needed today to stay in this place of waiting.

My children have endured a lot when it comes to Mom and Dad being involved in their love lives! The girls have not loved the fact that we ask this of the guys who want to date them. Even if it's just one date to a formal event, Dad gets to interview the guy. (One of them went home and told his parents, "Uh, yeah. I'm pretty sure Mr. Gresh just told me he'd kill me if I hurt his daughter.")

No doubt, the Gresh girls had moments when they did not like our involvement in their dating. They have to endure their dad's "pre-date" interviews of their guy friends, could not one-on-one date at all until they were graduated or about to graduate from high school, and had to share a full itinerary with us prior to each date.

I wish the same rigid involvement for you from your parents. I can see your eyes rolling now. Hang with me.

Embracing your mother and father's involvement in your dating—or at least accepting it—is a vital secret in your pursuit of a lifestyle of purity. I did not realize this until I began to minister to young women and saw a very specific pattern. Girls who were close to their families and closely monitored by their families, especially their fathers, had a special strength to live a lifestyle of purity. Girls who were not close to their families and were not closely monitored by their families, especially their fathers, had a bent toward sexual curiosity and activity. That is not true 100 percent of the time, but it is in the majority of cases.

Even if you are somewhat close to your parents, you may feel tied down by their rules and at odds with their preferences. That's OK. What you are going through is called "individuation" or simply becoming independent. But the danger is that you will try to pull away completely before you have the experience and wisdom to protect yourself. Your parents' rules are built upon love and a knowledge that you do not have. I want to encourage you, maybe convince you, to lean into their involvement. Of course there are the obvious reasons, like the fact that they probably know you better than you know yourself in some ways. They deserve to be honored just because God says they do. But I see two vital reasons to embrace your parents' involvement in your dating life specifically as it relates to the issue of purity.

YOUR FATHER CAN FILL THAT SPECIAL GUY-SHAPED HOLE IN YOUR HEART

I know a wonderful man who has an exceptionally close relationship with his daughters. He told me that one day his teenage daughter suddenly asked, "Dad, why am I not totally boy-crazy like some of my friends? I mean, I like guys, but I don't seem to *need* them like some of my friends do."

Without hesitation, he answered her, saying, "Because right now, I am doing everything I can to fill that guy-shaped hole in your heart. So you don't need a guy."

I like that answer.

Let me get right to the point: *Girls who lack a positive father/daughter relationship are very much at risk to be sexually active.* David Blankenhorn in a book entitled *Fatherless America* wrote, "Many studies confirm that girls who grow up without their fathers are at much greater risk for early sexual

Best MOTHER/ DAUGHTER Event!

The Pure Freedom Mother/ Daughter event is a night of girls-only fun for moms and their teenage daughters. We dig deeply into God's Word to discover truth about purity, beauty, and modesty. We worship. And we have a lot of laughs as we play obnoxious rounds of "Let's Make A Deal." Come see me at one. Or bring the event to your church. Visit www.purefreedom.org.

Best FATHER/ DAUGHTER Event!

OK, I do know this is about as good as it gets. High in the mountains of Northern California, there is an amazing place of God called JH Ranch. You can take your dad there to experience the Father/ Daughter Adventure, and what an adventure it is! Rodeos, rock climbing, white-water rafting, jumping and climbing from waterfalls, and lots of father/ daughter "solo" time to talk and grow. It's worth every penny, every mile it takes to get there, and every moment your dad is going to miss of work. GO! Visit www.JHRanch.com.

REBECCA ST. JAMES
on Dads

DANNAH: *What are some things you have done to strengthen the bond between you and your father?*

REBECCA: It is kind of interesting that you ask about that. My dad and I are really close because we work together. He is my manager, and some have asked, "Well, isn't that strange working with your dad?" But I think it is really good because he really understands me and is looking out for my best interest even more than any manager ever could. There have been times where I felt like I wanted more from him, and I think sometimes I expect too much. Especially as I get older . . . I expect him to kind of give me that support that maybe what I am longing for is the love or support that will come from my future husband. Sometimes my expectations are too high. I have to be careful. But if my expectations are legitimate and I am not expecting too much, I go to him and be honest about how I am feeling. I say, "Dad, this is a need in me" or "Dad, you really hurt me when this happened." We just make up about it, but that's hard to do. 'Cause I revere my father and respect him so much, so sometimes I am a little scared of going to him like that. But I think it is really important to go to him when you've got hurt like that.

After many years of faithfully waiting in purity, Rebecca St. James wed Jason "Cubbie" Fink in 2011.

activity, adolescent childbearing, divorce and a lack of sexual confidence." [1] I have seen this confirmed in many sources. In fact, in one study of the sex lives of a hundred teenage girls, the girls actually admitted that they often "swapped sexual encounters for the fathering they felt they weren't getting." [2] I don't want to push too many statistics at you, but that's a little scary since many of you don't even have the privilege of living with a father in the same house and those who do live with a father often find that relationship frustrating. [3]

When I was small, my father and I were very close. I was his little dog-training companion, often traveling with him on weekend trips to dog shows. He called me Sally. (I have no idea why, but it was like our secret love language.) He was always pinching me as if he could not get enough of me. It was really a neat little relationship. When I hit seventh grade, it was like a great big wall went up between my dad and me. Some of it was his fault. Some of it was my fault. I became withdrawn and quiet in an effort to begin to build my own world. It was very painful for both of us. The worst of it lasted until I went away to college, when we both began to realize how very much we missed each other.

I think sometimes dads become afraid of their daughters' changing bodies and begin to feel awkward about how they communicate with their little girls. One author wrote, "How puzzling it must be for a girl who has been used to being daddy's little girl, to snuggling in her father's lap and being tucked in at bedtime, suddenly to find her father pulling away. 'You are too big for that now,' her mother or father tells her. Too big for family hugs? Too big for paternal love? 'It feels like you did something wrong,' one teenager explained when talking about how her father started distancing himself."[4]

You must crash through that wall sometime. It won't necessarily get easier, and you never stop desiring a loving relationship with your dad. Your relationship with your father is, perhaps, never as important to you as during the teen and early adult years when, for many, it seems to be so tough to enjoy.

I'll give you some practical ideas for that father/daughter relationship in a moment. While I am trying to convince you of the need to embrace your parents' involvement in your dating relationships, I'd like to tell you the special thing that your mom can bring to the table.

YOUR MOTHER HAS THE ABILITY TO VACCINATE YOU!

You remember that little red lizard and the little monsters we talked about in chapter 6, "Purity Is a Process"? Well, I believe many times they are inherited. From the families of alcoholics are born alcoholics. From the families of liars are born liars. From the families of sex addicts are born sex addicts. Ask any Christian psychologist or counselor. They will tell you that they see this pattern every day. It is also present within the Bible. For example, we know that David had a weakness for women. His sin with Bathsheba led to more sin in the form of murder. Solomon, David's son to Bathsheba, carried on the family iniquity. Solomon had seven hundred wives and three hundred concubines. Many of them were "foreign" women who did not believe in God. God clearly told Solomon not to marry them. Solomon had the same tendency toward sexual sin that his father, David, displayed.

Look at it like this: When you were ever so small, your parents knew there were certain diseases that you could catch such as polio and German measles. Because these can be deadly or cause severe damage to you, they chose to take a tiny amount of this sickness and inject it into your perfect little body. They knew that if your body was aware of this disease, it could learn to fight it.

It is much the way with diseases of the soul. The same diseases or sins that your parents came up against in their life will very likely be the ones you struggle with as well. If you can be given a taste of that through their testimony—and perhaps seeing their shame and regret—you will be better able to fight against it.

So, how do you fix a rough relationship with your dad or mom? How do you get comfortable enough with your mom and/or dad to embrace their involvement in your dating life? It can be a long and difficult process, but I have a few simple ideas to get you started.

Recording Artist
STEPHANIE SMITH on
Fatherlessness

DANNAH: *What would you say to girls growing up without a dad in their lives?*

STEPHANIE: Growing up fatherless was hard. I was reminded of my dad every time I looked in the mirror because I was tall and I got my height from him. There were no birthday cards or even a token twenty-dollar bill at Christmas. I had never heard my father's voice over the phone, saying hello. I may not have understood all of the reasons my father left, but the hard fact that he wasn't there affected my life. Although I struggled for a long time, I knew that I would never be at peace until I had learned to forgive him through the grace of Christ. Forgiveness is a powerful thing. Often we think it means putting our tail between our legs and shrugging our shoulders as we try to convince ourselves that what happened didn't really matter. But forgiveness is just as much for the person offering it as it is for the one it's being offered to. It was hard, but I chose to forgive my father. I also made another choice and that was to believe the promise of my heavenly Father when He said, "A father to the fatherless . . . is God in His holy dwelling. He gives the lonely a home" (Psalm 68:5–6). The statistics on children from broken homes are alarming. But if you are one of those children, don't see yourself as a statistic. Know that you were created and seen by God before the beginning of time. And accept His offer to defend, protect, and love you and call you His son and daughter.

WRITE A LETTER

One of the things that I have seen have a great impact is letter writing. I wrote many letters to both of my parents when I was in junior and senior high school. It always seemed to readjust both my attitude and their response to me. As I wrote, I often found that a lot of what I expected from them was selfish and demanding. I was able to go back through the letter and edit it before I gave it to them in final form. It was a good exercise in examining my own attitude. As I edited, only the legitimate concerns made it through to the end. With my selfishness out of the way, my parents were able to see my point, and we often came to a good understanding.

Ron Hutchcraft recommends this kind of communication too. He says that a letter is "usually better said, better heard, and better remembered." He has often seen a simple letter transform families.[5]

Writing a letter is something that I particularly recommend if you are struggling with your relationship with your dad. Even if you are not struggling with the relationship, it is vital that you pursue an open relationship with him. Won't you sit down right now and write a letter to your dad? Express to him how much you crave his affection. Maybe tell him some of what you have felt God telling you as you read this chapter. Tell him how vital the father/daughter relationship is for you. Tell him you love him. If the relationship is strained, tell him you feel hurt by the wall between you and ask him to be your hero and to come crashing through it to find you again. Go ahead. Give it a try. Recognize that your dad is a very important element in your journey to live a lifestyle of purity. Oh, you can do it without him, but it is easier with him walking beside you.

LOOK FOR **YOUR DAD'S LOVE LANGUAGE**

Men are so different from women that there was once a bestselling book titled *Men Are from Mars, Women Are from Venus*. Why did it sell so quickly? Because nearly every woman could identify with trying to talk to the man of her dreams and feeling as if he was talking in some language so foreign it had to be from another planet. Well, guess what? Dads and daughters have a hard time talking the same language too.

A wise friend of mine, who has raised three wonderful, now-grown children, told me this secret. She said that often when her husband and daughters communicated, the girls had a hard time seeing his love. So she taught them to look for his love language.

As soon as she told me this little secret, I could see my dad's love languages all over the place. He and I did not hug and kiss and touch a lot. We did not go on "dates." We were hardly ever alone for quiet talks, but he loved me in his way. When I turned in a science project in high school, it was always one of the best because my dad would spend hours and hours painting solar panels, photographing dogs' noses, or covering display boards in felt. If I called him from college with a question about how to study, he would talk forever. I had and still have this notion that my dad can fix absolutely anything I break because he always, always has.

You might not feel your dad's love. The fact is, you might never easily see it in the language that you would like him to speak. But look for it. Look hard. Don't expect him to try to speak your love language. Identify how he says, "I love you" and accept it as his own unique love language.

CONFIDE IN YOUR **MOTHER**

I don't run into quite as many of you struggling with deep issues in regard to your mom. Probably the most frequent issue is that she might not be communicating as effectively as you might like. You may feel like she isn't *really* hearing you, especially on the issue of relationships. The majority of you have stated that you'd like to talk to her about issues of sex.[6] Although your mother is the parent who will be most likely to communicate with you about sex, the two of you often have a great big communication gap. In one study, 75 percent of the mothers felt like they were communicating very directly and effectively with their daughters when it came to sex. Only half of the daughters agreed.[7]

So, what's the problem?

While you are discovering, deciding, and searching for answers to your own issues of sexuality and purity, you are resurfacing the discovering, deciding, and searching she did when she was your age. She has been right where you are and knows exactly how you are feeling. She once struggled with waiting to give her heart to someone just like you are waiting right now. It is never easy, but it could be easier for you if you lean into her wisdom.

Your best bet at benefitting from her wisdom is to be honest with her about the level of emotional and physical involvement you have with guys. (Hopefully not much if you aren't of marrying age!) I say that cautiously because each mother/daughter pair will be different, and you might have a mother who is really hard to talk to on this level. But don't assume that will be the case—try it. I am confident that most mothers would feel blessed for their daughters to confide in them about their dating life. When it comes to communicating about sex and dating, remember that purity speaks boldly. This is a good time to put that into practice. Tell her where you are. You might be surprised at what it will do.

I wish I had done this much earlier with my mother. I was probably seventeen when I really started to ask her advice about guys. My mother and I are both "pleasers." That can make the dating thing tough. I spent hours talking with my mom to help me make it through my craving to give my heart to Bob during the long season that God called me to give it to Him. During that time she told intimately how she struggled with many of the same things and what the cost of giving in to that struggle turned out to be years later. It gave me a resolve to carry on with the pure, slow burn. I absolutely could not have done it without her, and I desperately wished I had embraced her wisdom and advice years earlier.

With my mom's incredible patience and guidance, I managed to wait a long time for God to strengthen my love for Him. When God did finally give Bob and me a release to be together again, it was unbelievably worth the wait.

"**A**re you feeling OK?" I asked Bob.

"Yeah," he answered unconvincingly.

We sat in H&R Dairy eating burgers and fries. Well, I was eating. He was gagging with every bite of his french fries. His burger sat getting cold.

I was glad that our friendship was back on track. It was a sweet gift from God, which we had waited painfully to receive. I still longed for so much more, but at least we had both felt the release to be together again, and over the course of the past few months, we had built some of our best memories. We'd had to change tires in the rain on our way to his junior/senior banquet in Cincinnati. We'd had lots of long, intimate talks in Wittenberg Library. He'd taken me to Yellow Springs and spent the afternoon photographing me like I was a model. He was everything I had dreamed of and hoped for, in part because waiting at God's feet had made him more patient, more sensitive, and more romantic. (That was a definite plus!)

I was afraid of the next few months though. Tomorrow he would graduate. Monday he would start a job and would be a bachelor living eight hours away from me while I took another year to finish college. Oh, it felt like the waiting was going to start all over again.

One hour later, I was looking back across the audience of about two thousand college students and parents in Cedarville College's chapel. My friend Donna Payne had told me that Bob's "Senior Night," the dramatic stroll down memory lane that was a tradition the night before graduation, was highly formal. She'd convinced me to wear my soft silk dress, but I couldn't see a stitch of silk, lace, or anything close to formal in the house.

The lights went low and I watched as the class of 1988 portrayed some of their funniest moments. Then, out on the stage came Bob with Christine.

Wait a minute, I thought. My heart started pounding as I thought to myself, *He was supposed to be on costume duty. I didn't think he had an onstage part.*

They made small talk and then . . .

"Well, Bob, when are you gonna pop the question?" asked Christine.

"The question?" he answered nervously. That french fry gag seemed to be still getting the worst of him.

"Yeah," she pushed. "You and Dannah have been together a long time. Don't you think it's about time?"

My heart started pounding so loudly within me that I was certain everyone in my row could feel the vibration.

"Yeah, yeah," he said casually. "It is about time, but I had always dreamed of asking her somewhere with lots of friends and maybe even family present. You know, share in this great moment of joy. I'd want it to be just perfect."

"Well," she pushed, "why don't you show me what your version of just perfect would be like?"

"First," he answered as she faded offstage. "I'd look into my pocket to see if I had the ring." He pulled a black velvet box from his pocket as the audience rustled in awe.

"Then, I'd look for her in the audience," he said, walking off the stage toward me.

"Then, I'd take her by the hand," he said as he reached for me. As he walked me to the stage, I felt as if I was floating behind him. As I reached the stage there was a chair in front of me, which I collapsed into since my knees seemed to have forgotten how to bend. He knelt before me and looked into my eyes. Then he presented the box and opened it. The spotlights caused the diamond, which was surrounded by six beautiful sapphires, to glisten against the black velvet.

"Dannah Barker," he asked. "Will you marry me?"

Silence.

Time stopped.

His eyes.

His smile.

His heart laid so humbly before me.

It was my line and I knew what to say, but the emotion of this moment was welling up within me. How could I speak?

"Oh yes," I exploded with a smile and a giggle as our emotions were quenched in a strong embrace. As we walked offstage, the audience went wild, adding joy to this moment. I noticed for the first time members of my family and his, beaming with joy from the corner. Their cheers, encouragement, and wisdom had brought us to enjoy this most beautiful moment with them. It was a moment that could not be ruined or robbed by poor choices. The pure, slow burn had paid off. My prince was here and the sunset was creeping up over the horizon. April 29, 1989, was soon determined to be the day that we would ride off into it.

the truth about sex:

it's out of this world

Erin Davis on God's Gift of Sex

It started out as nervous giggles and erupted into head back belly laughter. There we sat on the corners of our bed in our tiny honeymoon suite, still wearing our wedding clothes without a clue what to do next. Our commitment to a loving and holy Savior, and more important His commitment to us, had kept us pure, helped us save this moment for each other.

What began as nervous uncertainty soon evolved into a passionate exchange of gifts. My gift to my husband and his gift to me was a level of intimacy reserved only for each other. As husband and wife, our offering to our Savior was a commandment followed, a commitment honored. We didn't expect it, but we soon realized that His gift to us was more than we ever could have imagined. As we lay nestled together listening to the waves crash against the shore, my groom whispered, "We are one," and I felt a peace and comfort that I had never known envelop me. We still giggle with joy at the thought of the gifts God has given us and stand amazed at the rewards that come with walking the path Jesus has paved for our marriage and ministry.

Erin Davis, Missouri

Erin was one of the first women Dannah Gresh ever mentored. Today she's passing on the flame of mentoring as a Christian author. She appears as a lead teacher at some of my events!

the truth about sex: it's out of this world

Understanding the Heavenly Purpose of Sex

I present my body as a living sacrifice that is
holy and acceptable. This is only reasonable in light of what
You have done for me! (response to Romans 12:1)

I lay with my body wedged into my new husband's, amazed at the gift of our first experience together. It was tender and fulfilling, proof of our love. It was awkward and unperfected, proof of our innocence. Never, in all my life, had I felt this warm and comforted as if the world had stopped around me simply so that I could really know and feel this moment.

Bob began to move away from me.

"No, don't go," I murmured, drawing him back to me.

He turned and kissed me tenderly on my nose, then proceeded to get out of bed. He tenderly and tightly wrapped me in the blankets and then knelt beside me.

"Dannah, I want to pray," he said. "I want to thank God for this gift and beg His blessing upon our marriage bed that we might always protect it."

There in the night with the moonlight shining a ray of light across our honeymoon bed, we praised the great God of the universe for our wedding night.

How can I even start to rearrange the meaning of sex in your mind? What you are exposed to on a daily basis is destructive to sex as God intended it to be. And much of what you see isn't even close to reality. The average person between the ages of two and eighteen sees 14,000 sexual references, innuendoes, and jokes each year on television. Fewer than 175 of those deal with the real issues of pregnancy/birth control, abstinence, or sexually transmitted diseases.

On the most popular evening shows that most teenagers watch, the conversation deals with sex 29 to 59 percent of the time. *Sex* is the most frequently used search word on the Internet, and even if you don't search using that word, you are likely to run into sexual content. The world makes sex seem common, casual, and cheap.

Yet we don't hear enough in church or private religious schools about how beautiful and honored sex is in God's eyes. Ed Young wrote,

> *Based on what is depicted by the media, any alien visitor to America would likely conclude that every person over the age of twelve is sexually active, that marriage is the last place to look for sexual satisfaction, that faithfulness is a nostalgic dream, and that even the sickest of sexual perversions is nothing less than every citizen's "inalienable right."*
>
> *This would be true, of course, unless they happened to visit the church. Then they would probably wonder whatever became of sex. They might never hear it mentioned at all—or perhaps only spoken of in whispers or condemning tones. Historically, to its shame, the church has either ignored the God-given gift of human sexuality or smothered it with an avalanche of "Thou shalt nots."*[1]

Stop right now. Quietly invite the Holy Spirit to reveal to you the truth of what my hands have typed. The truth that I am about to reveal to you is powerful, but not often spoken of . . . even in our churches. I want you to see it through God's eyes. Please stop to pray earnestly for God to speak to you.

Within the Scriptures, there are only four blood sacrifices. Before Christ came, God was honored and people showed repentance by the blood sacrifice of animals. And when God made His covenant with Abraham, He requested pain and blood through circumcision as an act of good faith on Abraham's part. By cutting away his foreskin, he demonstrated that his heart had gone through a change. (Ouch!) Those are the first two blood covenants.

The third and most magnificent is the atoning blood of Jesus, which is God's covenant to us that if we confess our sins, He is willing to erase them. (Thank You, Jesus!) The blood covenant of Jesus replaces the need to sacrifice animals and the need to practice male circumcision. Circumcision is still widely practiced, but mostly as a matter of cleanliness and health.

But wait, before you think, "Whew, I am glad I don't live in Bible times and have to practice animal sacrifice!" there is one left that God still asks us to practice! It was in existence in the Old Testament under the law, but in the New Testament it has new meaning and is the only blood covenant sacrifice God still asks that we practice today. My friend, it is your sexuality.[2]

In Bible times, a bride and groom were presented with white linens for their wedding night. They were expected to sleep on them, and the bride was expected to bleed on them as proof of her virginity. You see, God created you and me with a protective membrane, the hymen, which *in most cases* is broken the first time that we have intercourse. When it breaks, a woman's blood spills over her husband.

Your sexual union is a blood covenant between you, your husband, and God.

In the Old Testament, Malachi 2:14–15 warns us not to break the covenant of marriage. God asks us to prize our virginity and hold it up as our only blood covenant to Him. Revelation 21:9 calls Christians "the bride, the wife of the Lamb [Jesus]." Before Jesus was ever born to Mary, the Jewish

WHAT IS A Covenant?

The word *covenant* is taken lightly these days. It is often compared to a contract, but a covenant is far more than a contract. You see, when we enter into a covenant with God, we are receiving the gifts He grants (such as sexual pleasure, unity, and the blessing of children in marriage) based upon our faithfulness to the covenant. We are also agreeing that if we break that covenant (like many do when they divorce or commit adultery), that we will lose the full blessings of that covenant. A covenant is an if/then agreement. If you are faithful to it, then you will experience the full joy of it. You cannot expect to know the full blessings of it unless you commit to it with all of your heart. Expect the fullest of blessings from your marriage covenant, my friend. Know that on your wedding day it is an unbreakable covenant, and purpose to be faithful to it.

marriage customs were a portrait of Christ's relationship to us—that is, those who have embraced Him as Lord and Savior.

When a young Jewish man had his eye on a bright-eyed Jewish girl, he went with his father to her father. At that meeting, the groom-to-be was expected to present some sort of payment for the bride. A cow or two, some currency of the day, or a promise of labor were some of the forms of payment. If the father of the girl found the payment acceptable, he agreed that the young man could have his precious daughter *if* he first prepared a home for her. Off the young man went to grab his hammer and some lumber. He built a separate home if he could afford it. If not, he added a special section to his father's home for himself and his new bride.

During the time that this young man was building, the bride had a special job to do. She was expected to be waiting—oh, not just going about her everyday chores and thinking about her groom-to-be. No, she was expected to be *waiting!* She was expected to have as lovely a dress as she could make or find by her side. She was to be cleaned and covered in aromatic oils. She was to be telling her friends of her groom's one-day arrival. At night, she was expected to have an oil lamp burning as a sign that she was faithfully waiting. The lamp *could not* go out. It was the sign that she was ready.

Her groom returned the moment he finished their home. There would be no delay. If it was 3:00 in the morning, so be it. He would sneak into her home with his friends, first checking to see if the oil lamp was burning. Then he awoke her and carried her through the streets, shouting and rejoicing that she was ready and he could provide for her. The night would be one of solitude for the new couple to consecrate their marriage, and then the sometimes weeklong celebrations began!

Do you see what I see? I know you must see how romantic this was, but do you see the portrait? Do you see Jesus coming to earth just like the young man first came to the young woman's house? Matthew 25:1–13 compares the way that the church waits for Christ to the way a virgin faithfully waits for her husband. Can you

The HYMEN

The hymen is named after the mythical god of marriage. It's a tiny little membrane, which surrounds but does not entirely enclose the lower opening of your vagina. The hymen has no known function and never grows back after it has been dilated or torn. In some very rare instances, a baby girl is born without one or a young girl's hymen can be torn through rigorous exercise or accidents.[3] Let's pretend that it never, ever existed. This does not erase the physical portrait that the sexual union portrays of the spiritual truth of Christ and His beloved church.

see Him paying for our lives with His blood on the cross like the young man paid the father? Do you recall His ascending into heaven where He went to "prepare a place" for you and me, much like the young man went to build the house for his bride? And someday, when we least expect it, Jesus will return for His church in all of His glory and those who call Him Savior will be with Him forever, like the groom came back to take his virgin bride to live with him for the rest of their lives. Yes! I love the romance of the Jewish wedding tradition, but I love the powerful symbolism even more.

Ed Wheat, a physician, wrote,

> *The sex relationship receives such emphasis in the Scriptures that we begin to see it was meant not only to be a wonderful, continuing experience for the husband and wife, but it also was intended to show us something even more wonderful about God and his relationship with us. Ephesians 5:31, 32 [KJV] spells it out: "For this cause shall a man leave his father and mother, and shall be joined unto his wife, and they two shall be one flesh. This is a great mystery, but I speak concerning Christ and the church." Thus, the properly and lovingly executed and mutually satisfying sexual union is God's way of demonstrating to us a great spiritual truth. It speaks to us of the greatest love story ever told—of how Jesus Christ gave Himself for us and is intimately involved with and loves . . . those who believe in Him.*[4]

Oh, do you see what God has entrusted to you? The young bride who enters into her marriage a faithful virgin can celebrate wholeheartedly. (And I am not just talking about technical virginity. I am talking about a pure virgin whose mind is as pure as her body.) What great joy to be able to enter into a covenant relationship with a man on your wedding night with no memory of having that covenant marred! I cannot think of any greater earthly joy.

Perhaps you feel a bit left out because you do have some memories that will be tough to erase on that night. Well, my friend, I share that pain. I cannot say that the consequences have

The concept of marriage being a picture of Christ and the church has been my consuming passion. For ten years, I researched the hidden language of romance in the Bible and wrote a book called *What Are You Waiting For: The One Thing No One Ever Told You About Sex*. It's for college-aged women. I hope you'll read it if you're as intrigued with the sacred purpose of marriage as I am.

not been quite hurtful, but I can say that we serve a loving God who can mend every broken heart. If this truth hurts, I am sorry, but please keep reading and know that God is forgiving. I have some special encouragement for you at the end of the next chapter.

Covenants within Scripture were always "if-then" agreements. *If* Abraham would practice the covenant of circumcision, *then* he would be blessed with a great legacy of generations that followed God. *If* Old Testament characters would practice the blood covenant of sacrificing animals, *then* God would see their faith and forgive their sins. *If* Jesus shed His blood for our sins and we accept and embrace Him as Savior, *then* we could be forgiven and someday enter into heaven. So, you're asking, what's the *then, if* we wait until our wedding night to share in the sexual union with just one man?

Read on, my friend, and see that His blessing back to us comes in the forms of three lovely gifts.

WRITE YOUR STORY. In the Old Testament animal sacrifices were made for atonement and for praise. Today our bodies are to be *living* sacrifices (Romans 12:1–2). Stop a moment and read Psalm 63:1–8 and offer up your body as a sacrifice of praise to God. As David writes about each body part and praises God with it, give Him that part of you. Focus especially on verse 1 where he talks about his flesh yearning for God. Pray that into your life to replace worldly passions. Take this time to praise Him with your purity!

the truth about sex: getting down to earth

Lauren Webb-Beckner on Waiting

I had been a Christian for three months when I attended a tiny little weekend retreat led by a young woman named Dannah Gresh. I was dating the guy who'd led me to Christ. It never occurred to me that his desire to have sex was out of sync with God's plan. But on that retreat I learned that God had a different path for me and I had the choice to walk it or to ignore it. Thankfully, I'd never given in to the pressure to have sex, and I broke up with him immediately. It wasn't easy. My heart broke, and there were times I would want to run back to him. Dannah would encourage me that God had a better plan. And He did.

When I was a freshman in college, I met a guy named Kevin Beckner. He was an amazing, godly guy. He told me that he wasn't going to even kiss his bride until they were at the marriage altar. I said, "Good luck finding that girl!" But over the years our friendship grew.

One weekend, I went to Colorado with some girlfriends. Unknown to me, it was a setup. I was walking along the base of this majestic mountain near a crisp cool lake when who do I walk into but Kevin. Right there in the most beautiful place you can imagine, he proposed. It was more romantic than I could have imagined.

Lauren and Kevin Webb-Beckner, pictured with Dannah in St. Louis, Missouri

Lauren was the first young woman I ever mentored. We've stayed in touch through the years and on July 5, 2003, I attended her wedding, where I witnessed that first kiss!

the truth about sex: getting down to earth

Preparing to Enjoy the Earthly Gift of Sex

I belong to my lover, and his desire is for me.
(Song of Songs 7:10)

T*wenty of us sat in our pajamas in a circle with candles glowing at my purity retreat. God had given me this delightful opportunity to show girls how to make it to their wedding night without regret.*

Jenny's cotton pj's looked as soft as her creamy, white complexion. Her dimples chiseled a bit deeper into her cheeks as she chattered on and on with delight. She was giving a fantastic testimony about how she came to her marriage bed a virgin—physically and mentally.

"I dated a guy for four years. He was sexually active frequently before we dated. And we even got engaged, but I told him I would not participate in that," she remembered, a sense of gratitude coming through in her voice. "The relationship brought a great deal of pain when he broke up with me. I felt like I was going to be an old

RECORDING ARTIST
Rebecca St. James
on waiting

DANNAH: *Was it worth the wait?*

REBECCA: Yeah! It was so amazing to go to our honeymoon guilt-free—to come to that marriage bed, with no guilt, no shame, but rather a freedom to explore this experience and this gift of God that we had never shared with anybody before. It really is truly, truly beautiful. We saw that absolute wonder of how God planned things to be and why in the Bible He instructs us to keep the marriage bed holy. There's a reason behind this stuff. It's for our good, protection, and the betterment of our marriage and lives.

DANNAH: *How have you and your new husband grown together spiritually?*

REBECCA: We were given for our wedding, a devotional book called *Night Light*, by Dr. and Mrs. Dobson. It was the biggest gift that anybody gave us. My husband, Jacob, actually led devotions the first morning of our marriage. The day after our wedding, he just got that devotional book out and started reading it, and it has been the biggest intimacy-building element of our marriage. It's so powerful and profound to seek God together every day. When we're apart from each other, we send each other the devotional responses to the questions that we have in our devotional book. We write them out like a digital letter. Now we have those to look back at in years to come.

spinster. One month after we broke up, he was in another sexual relationship," she said matter-of-factly.

She communicated her great sense of relief, but also a great deal of pain wondering what God could possibly have in store for her. Soon, she said, He brought Bryan into her path. Handsome, athletic, popular, and driven, Bryan was also a virgin. The relationship escalated quickly into a vibrant partnership for Jesus. Her love for singing and his love for playing the trumpet complemented each other.

"Someone got me a copy of a good Christian sex book right before we got married," said Jenny. "I'd read this and I was like, 'Wow! Oh, I cannot wait for this.' I can remember reading parts of it out loud to my mom and dad and asking questions. There was simply no shame. I could not wait!"

Jenny's bright eyes twinkled with extra brightness as she talked about her passion for Bryan. "You know, we just might be having really lousy sex, but we have nothing to compare it to, and so we have a blast together," she said with a giggle.

Somehow, I thought, *I am pretty sure that Jenny and Bryan have glorious sex, and I believe it is because God has blessed their marriage covenant.*

I truly believe that when we keep that covenant by saving ourselves to love someone with all the intensity of our heart and body, He is able to bless us immeasurably beyond what we could have imagined within our sex lives. Bryan and Jenny were living that to the fullest, and it showed in her glow.

SEX IS GREAT FUN!

Like Jenny said, God made sex to be pleasurable beyond your wildest dreams. Proverbs 5:18–19 says, "May your fountain be blessed, and may you rejoice in the wife of your youth. A loving doe, a graceful deer—may her breasts satisfy you always, may you ever be *captivated* by her love!" (italics added).

Captivated! I love that word. Don't you love the idea of being the object of one man's desire to the point of captivating him? Josh McDowell told me that in the original language that verse read something more like this—"may you be intoxicated by her sex!" Whoa! So, that verse is all about being completely overtaken by the joy of sex with your spouse. God can do that for you. That blessing comes from being in God's presence and waiting for His timing for this gift of sexual union. Want proof?

Redbook magazine once published a survey conducted by Robert and Amy Levin. They took an in-depth look at the sex lives of 100,000 women. They labeled a portion of their respondents "strongly religious." "The strongly religious woman seems to be even more responsive than other women her age," they wrote. These women were more likely to experience "a higher degree of sexual enjoyment and greater frequency in love making experiences per month."[1]

On the contrary, those who fail to wait tend to face obstacles in learning to have fun in their married sex lives. In one book a male author says that he and his wife were virgins by God's grace when they got married, but they had been physical up to a certain point. Because of that sexual activity, they had trained her body to get to that point and stop. So, when they got married, it took them several years of reconditioning to teach her body to enjoy sexual intimacy and get to the point where they were blessed by the fantastic fun of the sex.[2]

Take It a Step
Further!

In a survey of 3,377 married couples by Tim and Beverly LaHaye, couples who prayed together regularly were 10 percent more likely to have a "very happy/above average" sex life than those who did not pray together.[3] Wow! God loves to be in the very center of a vibrant marriage relationship, and He blesses that with the great physical gift of sexual satisfaction.

I am not saying that sex outside of marriage might not have some pleasurable moments. But it's a poor substitute for the real depth of pleasure that can be experienced within a faithful marriage, and it can really water down the pleasure you have with your husband.

God is waiting to fill you with more blessing than you can imagine. Don't miss how much fun sex can be. *If you will wait, then* it will be exciting!

SEX IS FOR **MAKING BABIES!**

Giving birth was the single most fulfilling accomplishment of my entire life, and I have a hunch that it will not be equaled. I remember a particularly proud moment that came in a most humbling circumstance. One hour after my beautiful Alexis was born, I found myself naked in a shower being tenderly washed down by a nurse. It was wonderful. I felt so spoiled. (Everyone should get a sponge bath like this sometime in her life.) As the warm water trickled down my body, I recounted every little pain and every big, "ouchy" push. I could hardly stay on the ground as the pride bubbled inside of me at the thought of a little girl to take home to my adored toddling boy. There was not one modest bone in my body at that moment. I remember wanting to open the door to invite everyone in for a peek and to scream, "Do you have any idea what *THIS* body just did! It is amazing!"

The God of the universe has given you the incredibly godlike gift of creating life. I don't think one person on this earth could actually begin to explain why or how one tiny round egg cell and one swimming sperm cell could turn into a vibrant life, but through the gift of sex it does happen.

Of course, you can make life whether or not you are in the covenant of marriage. But creating a life is the most incredible thing you will ever do. It deserves to be unmarred and undistracted by bad timing. *If* you will wait, *then* when you make new life, it will be with great celebration!

SEX **ENHANCES INTIMACY!**

When my husband and I enjoy the great gift of physical closeness, there is a difference in our relationship. We talk more. We help each other more. We hug more. We hate being apart. We can't wait to see each other again. We lie around and talk like we are college kids again. We dream. We confess. We laugh. We are consumed with each other as we go about our day, whether we are riding bikes with the kids, teaching a high school Bible study, or washing dishes. *We are one.*

Genesis 2:24 says that we should leave our father and mother and "be united" and become "one flesh."

That's hard to fathom, but couples who have purity within their marriage experience a distinct "oneness." What makes it even harder to understand is the casual approach to sex that much of today's social and political arena endorses.

Sadly, this gift is most at risk if you are sexual outside of marriage. In fact, I have frequently heard girls and guys talk about how sex outside of marriage really drove them apart rather than brought them together.

Plus, if you are sexually active before you are married, you may find yourself returning to memories with another sexual partner at a moment that should be for just you and your husband. What a sad thing to be robbed of those precious, private moments. Oh, guard yourself against that!

Intimacy starts with something in your heart, not with your body. But within the marriage relationship, sex really enhances and creates a new level of intimacy that can only be experienced between two fully committed, faithful, lifetime lovers.

In her effort to convince America to embrace abstinence and forget the safer sex message, Kristine Napier wrote, "Sex involves not just the sexual organs, but also the heart and mind. Teaching only the mechanics of sex and contraception ignores this. It ignores the concept that sexual intercourse is about total love and commitment, about sharing the singularly spectacular gift of oneself. . . . We must help [people] understand the human side of sex—the emotional and spiritual qualities that make it distinctly human."[4]

God loves to bless us. When we stay within the confines of His covenant, He loves to bless us in three ways.

If you will wait, *then* it will be a blast.

If you will wait, *then* you'll make babies with great celebration.

If you will wait, *then* you will be one. You will know a unity that few people have the privilege of tasting. You will understand the great mystery of how God can take two and make them one.

If you will wait . . .

then you will be blessed!

BUT WHAT IF
you have made
some bad choices
in your past?

"Your disobedience does not remove God from your life. It does remove God's blessing from your life." My former pastor, Tim Cook, said that this past Sunday, and it stuck. I realized that that time when I was mired down in a bad relationship, God was still there. But He is just and simply could not bless me. Oh, how He wants to bless us. And, oh, how He did bless me when I stood before Him and begged for forgiveness and healing. Want a really exciting example of how you might be restored? Rahab! You know, Rahab the prostitute! Rahab was one of the Canaanite people who were so sinful that God had condemned them to die. Her particular sin was sexual. But Rahab became a believer, and her life was spared when the land of Canaan was overtaken. But the story doesn't end there. She married an Israelite and had a son named Boaz, who had a son named Obed, who had a son named David. See it yet? Jesus was born out of the line of David. God saw Rahab's new, pure, clean life and claimed it to be in the family tree of Jesus Christ. Now that's a blessing! He wants to see you experience all of His blessing.

not you again, Satan!

Roseanna Thompson on Sticking to Her Standards

Before high school, I had always said that I wasn't going to date until I was sixteen. But in ninth grade after seeing other girls in serious relationships and beginning to like one of the boys in my class, I wasn't so sure about waiting. One weekend I attended a Pure Freedom retreat held by my church, and received a copy of *And The Bride Wore White*. Dannah's words rang true, and I started dreaming of a guy who was not just a Christian but on fire for God.

I have now turned sixteen and am approaching the end of my junior year. I have never dated, let alone kissed a guy, but it doesn't matter anymore. I have seen many of my friends lose everything in volatile relationships. This has made me realize that my decision to stay single is a smart move that will protect both my body and my heart. I can't wait to see who God will bring into my life in the future, but for now I am happy to remain single and unkissed.

Roseanna Thompson

not you again, Satan!

Facing the Consequences to Find Healing

"Psst! No one needs to know about this!"

God said to the snake, "Because you have done this, you are cursed more than any wild animal and you will crawl on your belly and eat dirt all the days of your life. I will put hatred between you and the woman—between your seed and her Seed. He will crush your head though you only strike His heel." And to Eve, God said, "You will have great pain in childbirth. And you will have an unquenchable desire for your husband who will rule over you." To Adam He said, "Because you listened to Eve, I curse the ground that you will painfully work to feed yourself. The ground will grow thorns and thistles for you and you will now have to eat the plants of the field. By your sweat you will have food to eat until you die. From the ground I made you and now to the ground you will return."...Then God made garments of skin for Adam and Eve and clothed them. (Genesis 3:14–19, 21, author's paraphrase)

T he lodge had been the perfect choice for this retreat. Pajamas, popcorn, and a hot tub were what I needed to leave behind the deadlines, management duties, and a dirty house.

Within twelve hours, I'd bonded to many of the dear women as we were challenged to reach deep within ourselves and find those things in our lives that still hurt. As the facilitator began to draw things to a close in the final session, she invited women to practice the principle of release. She invited them to truly start healing by confessing long hidden secrets. After a few minutes of awkward silence one woman stood.

"I was sexually active before I was married. My husband doesn't know."

The tears flowed.

"I had an abortion. It felt like my soul would never heal. Then, I had another."

"I have been in and out of relationships since I was thirteen. I am totally dependent on men."

"I never told anyone, but my uncle abused me sexually."

The women drew closer and continued talking and encouraging for hours.

Embraces.

Tears.

Healing.

Freedom.

I was seeing active, godly, churchgoing women in their thirties, forties, and fifties admit the secret sins—sometimes not even their own sins—that were still causing great pain after decades. Many of them were confessing sexual sins. Most of them were dredging up memories from their teenage years. As the session turned into hours of talking, hugging, and crying, I watched the countenance on these women's faces change into relaxed contentment. They would leave released from the blackmail Satan had been using to ransom their freedom.

I walked out onto the great ranch-style porch of the lodge and felt quite small as I looked out over the mountains cascaded with fall's rich tapestry. I pondered what I'd just seen.

Time had not healed these wounds.

Secrecy had not made them any less painful.

A simple, tearstained confession had helped these women move toward ending the imprisonment and the beginning of healing.

Some snake skeletons have little legs on them, as though the snake used to have legs. That may puzzle scientists who believe in evolution, but it does not surprise me. I am tickled with delight. God told us right in His Word that He removed the snake's legs because of how it had been used of Satan. The snake's consequences were the loss of its legs.

Know this. God is just and does not omit the consequences of our sin . . . like those skeletons prove.

Making poor sexual choices will bring consequences. I am not talking about pregnancy or AIDS or STDs. I am talking about the cancer that eats away at the heart.

God does forgive. As I told you in chapter 4, that forgiveness is immediate. But being forgiven is not the same as being restored or healed. Eve had to accept the consequences of her sin, which were to experience pain in childbirth and to have an unquenchable desire for her husband who would rule over or "be in charge of" her.

The very saddest consequence of sexual sin that I have seen is that the day does come when someone you know and love will need to hear your confession. For me that day came after five years of marriage.

JOSH MCDOWELL
on sexual healing

DANNAH: *How important do you think confession is to the process of sexual healing?*

JOSH: I think it is very critical. I am not sure a girl can truly experience God's forgiveness apart from her parents. She can't. God wants to express verbally—through Mom, Dad, an older sister, a pastor's wife, or someone like that— that He forgives them.

It had been ten years since I had given away the gift that God meant to be my husband's. During that decade, I had struggled with my self-image, my value in Christ, my sense of integrity. I had determined to tell Bob about my sin before he proposed to me, or at least before I answered his proposal. Then, he surprised me and proposed to me onstage in front of two thousand people in a more romantic way than I could have dreamed up myself. To say the least, it was a bad time to bring up my hidden past. Our engagement was filled with moments when I tried to tell him. And the first several months of marriage, I tried again. This hidden sin was robbing me of many moments of joy. I read book after book searching for permission to never tell him. Eventually, I kind of stuck the notion that anybody needed to know in a drawer, like you might a piece of junk.

Then one day, I was driving down the road with my brand-new baby girl in the seat behind me as I listened to a popular Christian talk radio show while a man and woman talked about raising sexually pure daughters. I only heard two sentences.

The Man: What is the number one question teenage girls ask their moms?

The Woman: Mom, did you wait?

My heart broke into millions of pieces at that moment. One day my Lexi would ask me that question.

That night, I sat for three hours in a dark bedroom with my husband until a tearstained confession could make its way out of my lips. At that exact moment and in my husband's tender arms, I felt release. I felt healing. I felt free.

During all those years of hiding, I had been like Adam and Eve in the garden, sewing together fig leaves. How pathetic! Those leaves may have camouflaged their shame, but I doubt they made them feel comfy and cozy. When God came to them and made them own up to their actions . . . *then,* the great God of the universe clothed them in garments of skin. If He had not done so, they might have spent the rest of their lives finding fresh fig leaves to replace the wilted ones!

If you think that no one needs to know about your sin, you are believing a great lie of Satan.

I never understood this completely until this summer when I was at a conference. As the leader read, "Confess your sins to each other and pray for each other so that you may be healed" from James 5:16, it all came together in my mind. God's forgiveness was immediate. The healing was something that would come more slowly and through the nurturing of other Christians as they verbalized to me God's loving forgiveness.

Oddly enough, as I slowly began to confess within the confines of close-knit Bible study groups and small gatherings of women, I found that many of them were also hiding in silence and fear from mistakes in their past. In my confession, they found the courage to confess and begin the process of healing too.

In other words, speaking about it frees you and others too! Don't let Satan's knowledge of what you have done blackmail you into silence.

I am not saying the whole world needs to know or that you have to write a book about it. (Can you believe God asked me to do this?) But find one person who is older and wiser and who is making right choices in her life and confess. After your confession to God, the most important people for any confession are the ones most directly affected. Your mom would be my first suggestion, but if that seems impossible to you right now, choose someone else to whom to confess and from whom to borrow courage and advice to someday go to your mom. Use great discretion in choosing someone and ask God for guidance, but don't waste any more years or months hiding.

purity
watches

burning
flames

LaDel Brown on The Pearl of Great Price

I hosted a retreat based on And the Bride Wore White *for 225 girls in my area. I felt that the session on giving up fake pearls for the Pearl of Great Price was something I needed to really focus on. Just a few months earlier, my mother-in-law had passed away and just before she died she gave me several strands of pearls.*

I asked her if she cared if I used them for the retreat, and she said, "Goodness no! You know, LaDel, it is not what we take out of this world that matters. It is what we leave behind that will make a mark on people's lives." I shared this with the girls, and as they sat and pondered what they would commit to give up by writing it on their "fake pearl" price tag, tears began to flow, and one by one they came up; as I tossed their price tag in the trash, I handed them a pearl from my mother-in-law. I miss her greatly but I know there are 225 girls with a part of her heart to keep them going in the right direction. Thank you, Dannah, so much for this wonderful material. I plan to do it again and again.

LaDel Brown, California

purity watches burning flames

Finding M.O.R.E. to Help You

Your path led through the sea, your way through the mighty waters, though your footprints were not seen. (Psalm 77:19)

"I need to be held," I confided in my husband.

"Then you come right here," he said, plopping himself on the sofa.

He wrapped his arms around me, engulfing me in his scent and his warmth. This was a safe place. I felt warm tears flowing down my cheeks as I relaxed into his embrace.

"You can think you are really good and that you have really tried to live a godly life," I stammered through my pain. "Then, you look back and realize you're not at all worth the chances you have been given."

Through the silence that followed, our hearts spoke. He knew my secret pain. Last night was the night we had planned together for many, many months. My heart's desire was, is, and always will be to live a lifestyle of purity, but in high school I detoured from that pursuit long enough to get tangled up by Lust. Like no other sin, moments of unbridled passion had intertwined my life painfully into another's. I had to make one final call to cut the last fraying cord. After fifteen years, I had called Michael to request forgiveness and to offer mine. It was a final act to sever the past, but it did not come without discomfort. Any moment of passion that was lustfully lived out in that youthful relationship was not equal to the pain that I felt searing my heart at this moment.

"Who am I to write this book?" I cried.

"Dannah," he said as he cradled my head in his hands. "Who else has this passion? Who else understands the pain? Who else is talking about the glory? Who else?"

"But . . ." I resisted.

"I was always held to a higher standard by you than by any other girl I ever dated. You were strong, uncompromised, and pure," he affirmed. "That's all I know of you. That's all that matters to me."

"But . . ." He pressed his hand to my lips.

I had worked for years to aggressively live a lifestyle of purity, but at this moment I felt the demons of Lust and Pride taunting me with memories they'd created just for me. I felt as if they'd brought legions of their cruel friends to surround my home.

But angels were fighting equally hard and were about to set the stage to win a battle in my life.

The telephone broke the silence. It was Meghan. She is one of "my girls." I met her on one of my retreats, and we are working together to build purity and contentment and wholeness into her life. It is not an easy battle. Bulimia and anorexia pursue her. A broken heart from a past relationship provides enough pain to bring frequent tears. I hadn't heard from her in weeks and was beginning to feel she might not need me for much more of her journey. Her call confirmed that she did.

"I have sooo much to tell you," she said. "I am doing great, but I really need to talk."

"How's Thursday?" I asked.

"It's a date," she said.

I crawled into bed with the knowledge that God was using me in spite of who I am, not because of who I am. This ministry is not about me. It is all about Him. Little did I know that in the morning following this dark hour, He would lovingly pour out His Spirit to affirm my usefulness, His omnipresent leadership, and your final secret.

--------------⟨3•⟩--------------

T hat was last night. I am actually in the middle of writing this book, but I know without a doubt that God wrote this chapter in my heart this morning. I confessed my sin again and admitted my feeling of inferiority. I thanked Him for Meghan's call to encourage me and opened my Bible to read my psalm for today. And there at the end of Psalm 77, verse 19's great truth was revealed to me like only God can do.

"*Your* [God's] path led through the sea, *your* way through the mighty waters . . ." (italics added).

The psalmist was writing of the Israelites' walk through the Red Sea, which was parted when Moses raised his hands. They were leaving a land of slavery to find God's promised land. The psalmist acknowledged God as the One who actually parted the seas even though it was through Moses' upraised hands. But then, he wrote, "Though your footprints were not seen . . ."

They missed God's footprints! They stomped right across them and never saw them! Oh, how sad. God allowed His own majestic footprints to be stomped out as clumsy Israelites made their way across the sandy water bed, craning their necks to look to make sure old Moses still had his hands raised high in the sky. God lovingly gave them Moses' living hands because He knew that was what they needed to walk in His footprints.

When I think of Moses, I think of the burning bush and the passion that it brought to his life. He took some of the power of God that he received at that bush and used it in the lives of other people. When I think of women in my life who were like Moses to me, I think of a burning, passionate flame.

How OLD? How WISE?

A Washington, D.C., based Best Friends program encourages fifth through ninth grade students to encourage each other to remain abstinent. It's working! In a 1990 follow-up survey, none of the Best Friends girls were sexually active as compared to 37 percent of a control group.[1] Remember, these girls were no older than ninth grade but were making a great impact on one another. One of the greatest mentors I know is a senior in high school named Lauren Webb. It seems every time I turn around I hear another girl in our youth group saying, "Well, Lauren told me to . . ." They take her advice and they let her hold them accountable. She is a great burning flame. Older and wiser can be a matter of a few short years. Just make sure she is making right choices in her life. This isn't about having another friend. It's about having a leader.

I thought of the women through the years who have encouraged me and led me out of barren lands . . . sinful lands . . . boring lands . . . hopeless lands . . . old lands. Some offered words of encouragement. Some chastened me. Some forced me out. But always at pivotal points in my life, there has been a "Moses" to be my burning flame. I thought about the times when I was stuck or when I entered into a bad land and noticed the lack of anyone significant influencing my life. I noticed isolation prior to my bad choices to live stuck in a place where God did not want me to be. I reached for my journal and wrote a silly little poem about my burning flames and how I needed them.

I sat pondering Moses' role as a burning flame. Then, God gave me MORE! I reached for my *Experiencing God: Youth Edition,* which our youth group is studying right now. Guess who week 2, lesson 2 is all about? Moses. (Isn't God's timing wonderful!) It starts out, "Who delivered the children of Israel from Egypt? Moses or God? God did. God chose to bring Moses into a relationship with Himself so that He—God—could deliver Israel."[2] Wow!

It wasn't about Moses.

It was all about God.

This book isn't about me.

It is all about God.

Oh, I hope that you have begun or continued a journey toward God's promised land of a fantastic sexual union. There is probably one man who is waiting to be one with you, just as you wait to be one with him. I hope that I have been a burning flame in your life to give you the passion to follow the majestic footprints of God.

But soon you will close the pages of this book and will no longer see my burning passion.

Find a burning flame.

Don't do it tomorrow or next week. Ask God for guidance right now and find a burning flame in your life to look to for guidance and encouragement.

SHE SHOULD BE **M.O.R.E.**

. . . **M**aking right choices (living righteously) in her current life

. . . **O**lder and wiser

. . . **R**eadily accessible so she can watch you and you can watch her

. . . **E**xcited to burn for you

WRITE YOUR STORY. Grab your journal and write down a few names of people who have burned brightly for you in the past. Jot down the names of some women that you know who are M.O.R.E. Choose one of them to approach. Write your request to God to put it on her heart to burn for you!

Find a burning flame, my friend.
And promise me that when someone else finds you . . .

. . . no matter how old you are

. . . no matter what clutter lies in your past

. . . no matter how busy you are

. . . no matter how inferior you may feel . . .

you
  will
   be a
   burning
   flame
    for
     her.

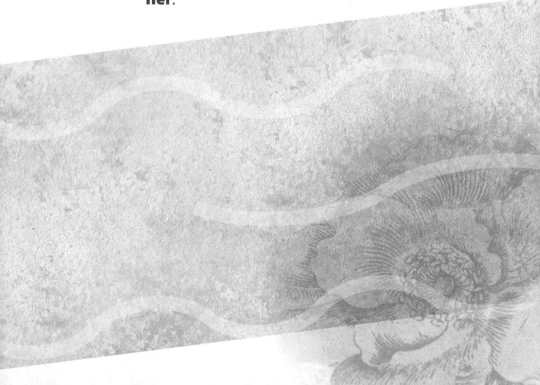

the payments on the pearl

continue

Carrody Miller on Using the Seven Secrets

Not long after I began to walk with Jesus at the age of sixteen, I met Paul. We fell for each other quickly, but after only two weeks of dating I felt like I was living a lie. The accumulation of past choices and mistakes weighed heavily on my heart. I knew that if Paul really found out who I was and what I had done, he would not want to be in a relationship with me. So, before both of our hearts got broken, I decided to tell him. I explained that I was not the pure, clean girl that he would want to marry someday and began to offer details about my past. But I was only three or four sins into my list before he stopped me. Looking into my eyes, he gently said that God had taken my sins as far as the east is from the west. He said that God had forgiven me and he did too. God spoke to me through Paul that day. I stopped believing that I was captive to my past sins, I was free and new and clean!

*The two of us committed our relationship to God and to purity that day. We dated for three years before Paul asked if we could take a break. I was heartbroken and soon realized that I did not know what my relationship with God was apart from Paul. Those nine months were hard and emotional but I grew enormously in my relationship with God. **And The Bride Wore White** was a tool that helped me give control of my life—including my relationship with Paul—to God.*

Two and a half years later I married him. In the moments after I had walked down the aisle, he played me a song he had written just for me.

"God up above is smiling down, our love is pure like you in your wedding gown.

Summer day in white, baby, take this life. Walk this road with me, in His hands we'll be."

Carrody Miller

the payments on the pearl continue

Using the Seven Secrets After Your Wedding Day

Though one may be overpowered,
two can defend themselves. A cord of three strands
is not quickly broken. (Ecclesiastes 4:12)

D*on't close this book and say, "What a rosy little life Dannah lives." There have been some really neat and romantic memories created in the first fourteen years of my marriage, but it hasn't been perfect. No marriage is without pain. Bob and I have made each other cry a lot. We've struggled to continue the pursuit of purity in both of our lives, and* sometimes we have failed. Once, the only thing holding us together was Jesus. I remember writing in my journal, "My cord is severed. Bob's cord is severed. Lord, You are the only cord in our 'cord of three strands' holding fast." (I think God liked that admission. He soon tied those severed spots into nice tight knots!)

Marriage is not easy. In fact, I am very thankful for the seven secrets that God gave me during my dating years. I still use them a great deal.

I still need to remember that *purity is a process,* because I still mess up and have to get back on track.

I still need to remember that *purity dreams of its future,* because it keeps my marriage fresh. (I have this really wild dream of a huger-than-my-wedding celebration for one of our special anniversaries . . . when we can afford it. Dreaming of that day keeps me falling in love with Bob. And silly as it may seem, I dream of us sitting on a porch in rocking chairs with great-grandchildren crawling into our laps.)

I still need to remember that *purity is governed by its value* or I might buy things at the store that I should not wear and I might forget to behave becomingly in front of my husband. (It is important to maintain some mystique!)

I still need to remember that *purity speaks boldly* so that I can keep Bob on track spiritually. He does the same for me.

I still need to remember that *purity watches burning flames.* I stick very close to my mom, Kay Barker, who is my favorite burning flame. Women like my friend Tippy Duncan have helped me to be faithful and make right choices in my marriage. I expose myself daily to burning flames who don't even know me, like author Becky Tirabassi, who convinced me that prayer could change my life. (It did.) I listen to Sara Groves every single day because her music teaches me to worship at the very throne of God. I've learned that not following the lead of burning flames is detrimental. So, I pursue them aggressively.

I still need to remember that *purity embraces wise guidance* because I am still learning who I am through my family and how that fits into who Bob is because of his.

But most of all, I need to always remind myself that *purity loves its Creator at any cost.* Now that I am in a covenant relationship with one man, my faithfulness to him is a portrait of my faithfulness to my Creator.

I am sitting in a condo one hour away from home right now. I have come to finish this book. I don't mind saying that it is also a nice break from seemingly insurmountable obligations that Bob and I are finding ourselves under right now. The past few weeks have been filled with tension as we seek to make it through some tight deadlines. Last night I spent an hour on the telephone "debating" with Bob whose fault it is . . . his or mine. We ended the conversation with prayer, but we both felt angry and agitated when it was over. This morning I went to God to tell Him how terribly selfish my husband is being. (Ha!) I was brutally honest.

"God, I am very angry at him. How can I fellowship with You when I am so sure he is wrong?" Then I opened up my Rebecca St. James's *You're the Voice* devotional, which I am going through with Lauren, one of the girls I mentor. My lesson today was entitled "You Then Me." It was about selfishness. I felt convicted. I was the one being selfish, so I called Bob to apologize. Somehow, our conversation turned into another irreconcilable debate.

I cried. There seemed to be no way to work it out.

"Maybe we should just hang up," I suggested as calmly as I could after a good fifteen minutes of getting nowhere fast. "I am only becoming more upset, and I really need to focus. I can't focus when we are not united."

There was a long pause.

"Dannah, I don't want to fight. We are united," Bob answered. "We both love the Lord, and we are equally committed to loving each other. Let's just forget the whole first half of this conversation. We will work this out."

And we did. Very quickly too.

Why? Because Jesus is the very center of our love life.

He was before we even knew each other.

He was when we were dating.

He always will be.

Our love for each other is merely a portrait of our faithful love for our Creator . . . the Pearl of Great Price.

Recently Bob slipped this note into my suitcase as I left to conduct a purity retreat.

Sweetheart:

You are my pearl of great price. I cherish every moment with you.
I cannot wait until tomorrow to spend the whole weekend with you.

I love you,
B

May our marriage and yours-to-come be a portrait
of your devotion for the Pearl of Great Price.

He costs everything.
He is worth the price.

Letters from the Heart

Seven Burning Flames Tell Their Stories and Their Secrets

A Special Letter on Sexual Abuse

DEAR ONE,

Think of your deepest, darkest secret. That one thing that makes your stomach churn and your palms sweaty when you imagine admitting it to someone. It's that one secret you intend to carry to your grave, if it doesn't kill you first. For too many, that secret is childhood sexual abuse. That was once my secret too.

I grew up in a small town. Many who knew me considered me the "perfect girl" from the "perfect family." I came from a happy Christian home, and I excelled as an athlete, student, artist, and leader. But my bright hazel eyes and my super-achiever persona masked a Nicole who was carrying the silent pain of childhood sexual abuse. And I was too afraid to tell.

I believe childhood sexual abuse is one of the best-kept secrets in our world today and I believe that breaking the silence is the key to healing. But it isn't easy. If you have been abused, sharing your secret may well be your biggest fear. I know how you feel. It took ten years for me to tell my secret. My stepfather, like many abusers, manipulated me into silence through threats. He told me no one would believe me and if anyone did find out about "our little secret," my mom would hate me, divorce him, and I would never see her again. I thought it was my responsibility to keep our family together and protect my mom, so for a long time I did what my stepdad wanted without saying a word. I felt as if I had no choice, and I was scared, confused, and felt trapped. I forced myself to believe that it wasn't that big of a deal and that it was better if I suffered through the abuse and remained silent.

I was fourteen when I finally told my mom what had been happening to me for the past ten years, and I knew it was the right thing to do no matter how complicated things became. Confessing that longtime secret released me from my past so I could finally embrace the future. It freed me from the pain and shame. Finding the courage to confess allowed me to heal and discover the life I had been longing for.

Since then, I have also discovered that I am not alone. See, secrets love the dark, and in that darkness it's easy to believe you are all alone. If you have a story like mine, I want you to know that this isn't your secret to keep. It's the secret of the one who hurt you. Even so, you may be afraid to open up, and I understand that. It takes a lot of courage to tell. But I also understand a couple of other things that can help you overcome your fear. First, I understand that courage isn't the absence of fear; it's the willingness to act in the face of fear and it enables you to tell your story despite your fear. I also understand that telling your secret will start you on a path toward healing and freedom:

It will help validate your experience and feelings.

It will help you understand your innocence and your abuser's guilt.

It will help you realize that you're not alone.

It will help you open up to others so they can comfort and encourage you.

It will help you experience healthy emotions and honest relationships.

It will help restore your trust.

It will help boost your self-esteem.

It will help affirm your self-worth.

It will help you be a source of comfort to others.

When we keep this secret hidden inside, sexual abuse leads to feelings of shame and unhealthy ways of coping with those feelings. Our shame is rooted in the lies we believe about ourselves, especially the lie that the abuse was somehow our fault. I believed this lie for many years and, as a result, felt dirty and afraid of what people would think of me if they knew the truth.

Somewhere inside, many abuse survivors feel unclean and unable to regain their lost purity. I've heard many young girls say things like, "I'm already damaged goods. Who cares what I do with my body now?" The answer is that God cares. If you were a victim of childhood sexual abuse, you need to know that you are not damaged goods. You are not alone. And what happened to you was not your fault. You didn't choose sex when you were abused. You were a victim. But you can choose now. You can choose healing. You can have healthy relationships and you can choose purity. I hope you make the right choice. You are worth it, and so is your future.

If you've chosen to deal with your pain in unhealthy ways, I know that you're doing what you believe you need to do to survive. But eating disorders, self-injury, addiction, and unhealthy relationships only perpetuate the abuse and pain you're trying to escape. This kind of coping won't ever heal your inner wound. It will only lead to more wounds that will require their own healing. You'll never stop relying on unhealthy coping mechanisms until you get real about the pain underneath. Dear One, I pray you'll find the courage to tell your secret. I pray you would begin the healing journey Christ has for you. Find someone you trust. Share your story. Write it down. Read it out loud. Cry! Yell! Get it all out! I believe the first step to healing is breaking the silence.

Find your voice, Lovely One. You deserve to heal. May the silence be broken.

With Love,

Nicole Braddock Bromley

Nicole Bromley is an international spokesperson on the issues of sexual abuse, rape, and trafficking. She is the author of *Hush: Moving from Silence to Healing After Childhood Sexual Abuse* and *Breathe: Finding Freedom to Thrive in Relationships After Childhood Sexual Abuse* and the founder of OneVOICE (www.onevoiceenterprises.com). She lives in Columbus, Ohio, with her husband, Matthew, and sons, Jude and Isaac.

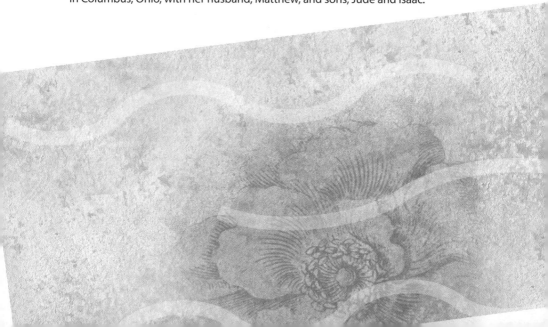

A Special Letter on Porn Addiction

DEAR FRIEND,

I know you don't know me, but I call you my "friend" because in a moment things are going to get real personal. My name is Crystal Renaud and for eight years I was addicted to porn.

How's that for an introduction? It's provocative, to the point, and 100 percent true.

Oh, and in case you missed it, I'm also a girl.

Perhaps you didn't know *girls* could be addicted to porn. Or perhaps you *are* a girl addicted to porn and thought you were the *only* one. Well, they can. And *you're* not.

I first saw pornography at ten years old when I found a pornographic magazine in my brother's bathroom. Instead of ignoring what I had discovered there, I opened the magazine and began to look through this new, very confusing material. My counselors have compared the emotional trauma of this first exposure to pornography to the emotional trauma of a rape victim. While that was a difficult parallel for me to accept, it was true. It was true because of how I reacted to that experience.

Reality was that I came in contact with pornography innocently. But the reality I believed was the shame I felt and the blame I placed on myself for looking at it in the first place. I realized I had an addiction when looking at my brother's stash and Dad's movie cabinet no longer provided me with the same rush it once had. Adding fuel the fire, I began to masturbate and view pornography online. This physical acting out combined with direct access to pornography led me to cyber sex and phone sex as well. The best part (as far as I could see) was that I got physical and emotional needs met while still carrying around my V card. Because ironically, being a virgin and being known for my virtue was important to me.

My acting out had become so secret and isolating that it was destructive to my life—relationally, emotionally, and of course, spiritually. I became a Christian at sixteen years old, and the severity of my addiction became impossible to ignore. I had countless unsuccessful attempts at stopping my behaviors.

Women are designed by God to need emotional intimacy. In my own life, pornography, and the behaviors pornography led me to, filled a huge need I had for intimacy, affection, and acceptance that I was missing from my dad. The relationship a girl has with her dad is vital to her emotional and spiritual life. Women will often see their heavenly Father in the same way they see their earthly father. And if what she finds from her dad is rejection, abandonment, or perhaps even cruelty, then she will believe God is the same way. If this sounds like you, then it is likely you are unaware of just how big the God-shaped hole in your heart really is.

Pornography use took me places I never thought I would go. It kept me there longer than I intended to stay. And it cost me more than I wanted to pay. I wouldn't come clean about my addiction until I was nearly nineteen years old. During a divine appointment, a woman I trusted shared with me her own past struggles with pornography use. It was through her confession that I was able to confess my own struggles and surrender this addiction to Jesus Christ and to a relationship of accountability with that woman.

My journey to sobriety wasn't flawless, but I'm happy to say that I've now been living in freedom longer than I was captive to my addiction. But it was a process. Recovery from addiction, any addiction, requires a healing of old wounds. Some wounds we are aware of while others have been buried so deep they've almost been forgotten. We must heal those wounds before we can truly become free.

I've comprised a process of steps using the word S-C-A-R-S. Just as the scars on Christ's hands and side proved who He was to Thomas, the scars left behind from our own wounds prove His healing in us. I want to share these steps with you, in hopes that you will find victory in whatever hang-ups you're facing:

S..... *Surrender;* Behavior modification doesn't work without surrendering control of our behavior to God. Surrender begins by asking the question, "Do I trust God enough to get well?"

C..... *Confession;* The word "confess" means "to acknowledge." Confession of sin is an acknowledgment of sin, with the intent of seeking forgiveness from God and others.

A..... *Accountability;* Be held accountable with the help of another person—not only to your actions but also to growing spiritually, becoming closer to and more intimate with God.

R..... *Responsibility;* By accepting responsibility, we begin looking at where our actions may have had an impact on others.

S..... *Sharing;* God never wastes an experience. Sharing is about knowing that you have a story and sharing it is an essential part of your healing.

I hope you haven't experienced what I have. But if you have, it's my prayer that through these steps and the healing power of Christ, you will find the freedom that He desires for you.

Blessings,

Crystal Renaud

Galatians 5:1

Crystal is the founder and executive director of Dirty Girls Ministries, where she has dedicated her life to helping women find freedom from pornography and sexual addiction. Her book *Dirty Girls Come Clean* is a great help if you are struggling with porn or know someone who is.

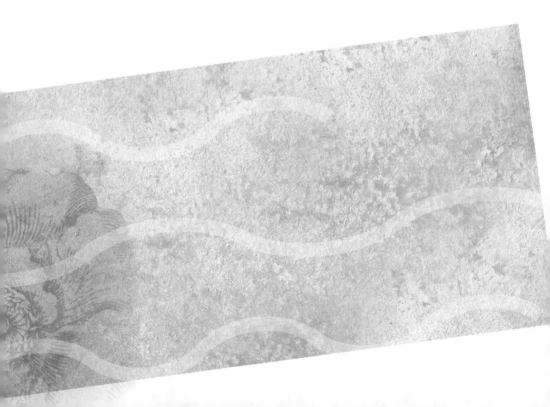

A Special Letter on Fatherlessness

HI FRIEND,

Many people know the unnerving fact that about 50 percent of marriages in the United States end in divorce, but not everyone is aware that 40 percent of children are growing up without their father's involvement in their life at all. I was one of them, raised just by my mom. Sadly, that's becoming an almost typical American childhood.

My parents' marriage was already rocky when I came along. When I was just six months old, my mother packed one suitcase for her, my older brother, and me, and we left for my grandparents' home. What was supposed to be a short getaway turned into the rest of our lives. I wouldn't see my father again for fourteen years.

Growing up fatherless was hard, and I was reminded of him every time I looked in the mirror. I grew fast. Literally. I was taller than classmates, friends, my older brother, and even some of my middle school teachers! My father is 6'4"—I got my height from him—but he wasn't around to put my heart at ease, assuring me that tall was beautiful or that standing out was okay. I just felt awkward. I was painfully shy, afraid to speak up, and other than being a head taller than everyone, I got lost in the crowd.

There were no birthday cards or even a token twenty-dollar bill at Christmas. I had never heard his voice over the phone, saying hello. I may not have understood all of the reasons for my father's absence, but the hard fact that he wasn't there affected my life. I finally met him when I was fourteen, something I had been dreaming about for years. Although my mother didn't speak of my father often, she never spoke harshly of him. We hadn't learned to fear or hate him. I was just curious. What would he be like? I was hopeful.

We were attending a funeral of a relative on my father's side, and although a little late, we had arrived before the ceremony began. As people stood around talking, I caught a glimpse of a tall man with glasses and thick hair. I slipped one arm through my brother's and gestured at my father with the other. He saw us and made his way to the back of the sanctuary where the three of us stood. I waited breathlessly as he greeted my mother and brother. "You must be Matthew," he said to my brother. Then he turned to me and added, "and you must be Priscilla." My heart hit the floor as I politely corrected him, "My name is Stephanie."

In one moment, all of my daydreams about him had come crashing down and I felt what it really meant to be fatherless. Disillusioned and depressed, I spent the next few years wrestling with anger and confusion. The reality that my father didn't care enough to even know my name, let alone know me, wasn't a wound I would recover from quickly. But although I struggled for a time, I knew that I would never be at peace until I had learned to forgive him through the grace of Christ.

Forgiveness is a powerful thing. Often we think it means putting our tail between our legs, and shrugging our shoulders as we try to convince ourselves that what happened didn't really matter. But forgiveness is just as much for the person offering it as it is for the one it's being offered to. Unfortunately, until Jesus comes back and restores our world, we will be dealing with brokenness. He knew that, so He taught us about the power and importance of forgiveness.

See, when someone hurts you, they place a burden on you, whether they mean to or not. Forgiveness is accepting that what happened hurt and that person committed a wrong against you, but choosing to release that hurtful action and that person to God. It was hard, but I chose to forgive my father.

I also made another choice to believe the promise of my heavenly Father when He said, "A Father to the fatherless, a defender of widows, is God in His holy dwelling. God sets the lonely in families" (Psalm 68:5–6). The statistics on children from broken homes are alarming. But if you are one of those children, don't see yourself as a statistic. Know that you were created and seen by God before the beginning of time. And accept His offer to defend, protect and love you and call you His son or daughter. Choose Him.

Love,

Stephanie Smith

Stephanie Smith grew up in State College, Pennsylvania, but moved to Nashville when she signed a contract with Gotee Records. She's released a full-length record and two EPs as well as a book called *Crossroads: The Teenage Girl's Guide to Emotional Wounds*.

A Special Letter
on Abortion

HELLO, FRIEND,

I want to invite you into one of the most private moments of my life. My decision in that moment defined my life into a before and after.

At the age of nineteen, life was good. I was the daughter of a pastor, attending a Christian college, and was dating the son of a pastor. I was carefree, enjoying both the newfound freedom of college and a dating relationship with a Christian guy. Even when my relationship with my boyfriend got intimate, I thought it was harmless.

But my picture-perfect world was suddenly shattered. I got pregnant. My boyfriend was less than supportive and told me that my life would be turned upside down if I carried the baby to term. He pressured and even taunted me by telling me stories of getting me kicked out of college. (The college expelled pregnant, unwed students.) He even used my greatest fear, that my mother would probably have a mental breakdown at the news, in order to convince me that I didn't have much of a choice.

I aborted my baby. There still isn't a day that goes by when I don't think about him.

I could have been engulfed in the most horrible grief imaginable, but I didn't have anyone to face it with me, and I wasn't willing to do it alone. I became numb and chose to tell myself that I made the right decision for that period of my life. But pain and grief kept threatening to resurface so I drowned out my feelings with drugs and promiscuity for many years.

Denial and distraction worked for a while, but ultimately I had to face what I had done. While it was the most painful time in my life, allowing myself to recognize that my child was a person and grieving him brought healing. And ultimately finding forgiveness in Christ was instrumental in finding peace and freedom.

Abortion has become a fiercely debated political, intellectual, and moral issue. But we can't lose sight of the fact that this horrible practice causes pain and sometimes even trauma to the mothers abortionists claim they are trying to protect. I am so much more at peace now than I was when I had convinced myself that I had only aborted a "blob of tissue."

Today, I am very loved by a wonderful husband, and I find tremendous fulfillment in a productive and successful career helping other women heal from abortion. What do I tell these women? First, I tell them that they are not alone. The Alan Guttmacher Institute (the research arm of Planned Parenthood, the world's largest abortion provider) recently stated that, if current trends continue, 43 percent of women in the United States will have had an abortion by the age of forty-five. Imagine that 43 percent of all women you know are postabortive—they sit in your congregation, work in your school, climb corporate ladders to success, and exist in every part of our society.

Second, I would have to say that a good step toward healing is confession. Oh, I had confessed my abortion before God, but confessing it to a loving, godly woman through sharing my testimony was a major step in my journey to healing. Telling this truth was one of the most frightening things I've ever done, but it was worth it. James 5:16 says, "Confess your sins to each other . . . so that you may be healed." God gave us each other to encourage and provide help in the process of healing.

I hope that you can't really identify with my story. But if you can, let me encourage you to tell an older, wiser, and very godly woman. If you don't feel you can talk to your mom about it right now, find a local crisis pregnancy center to talk to one of their counselors—they can be found in the "Abortion Alternative" section of your Yellow Pages and are equipped to help women who have gone through abortions. I know that sounds tough, but it will be very worth it. My prayer for you is that you would join me in the journey to healing.

If you are experiencing an unplanned pregnancy and considering abortion, know that abortion is *never* the solution. What is painted as a convenient choice that will help to keep you from derailing your life is a decision that is fraught with regret and pain. Remember, there is a person inside of you, relying on you. And you are not alone. Seeking out a counselor at a crisis pregnancy center will be a good choice.

And if you are that nineteen-year-old without a care in the world, please hear me. Premarital sex is costly. Even if you don't get pregnant, like I did, your heart is very precious and should be saved for the perfect man. One of my greatest regrets is that I couldn't share my innocence with my husband. Regardless of the fact that the "sky doesn't fall" when you go a little bit farther with your boyfriend than you would have liked, there are major consequences to your future. The boy who truly loves you will wait for marriage.

Always remember that God is a redeemer and, no matter what the choices you have made, is longing to forgive you and draw you close to His heart.

In God's Great Healing Love,

Sydna

A Special Letter on Passing It On

DEAR FRIEND,

I've learned a few things as I've journeyed through life and one of them is this: When God mends our broken hearts and sets us free, it's never simply for ourselves. It's to pass on to all those He brings into our lives! That's the incredible thing about God—He makes *all things* work together for our good (Romans 8:28). As we fall more in love with Him, we see it even more clearly.

Becoming a "burning flame" for those we come in contact with should not be something we take lightly, nor something we allow to pass us by. We need to be willing to share our stories so others can be set free with the love and forgiveness we've already received.

Healing isn't easy, but I believe that only the strong truly seek it. Walking through that process layer by layer takes total reliance on God. As much as I've wished healing could be an instantaneous thing, it never has been for me. It's not simply about surrendering the pain and brokenness; it's about being willing to walk *through* it with Him, allowing Him to be the Potter and reshape our hearts the way He knows best.

Throughout my journey, I had key mentors in my life, and one of them was Dannah. Until she came along, I couldn't express what I was going through. I was living in a prison, captive in my sin, afraid I would never be free. As I opened up to her about my pain, she taught me about the love of Jesus. She listened (though I was rather long-winded in my emails!), she was patient and loving, and she loved me the way I needed to be loved. With gratitude in my heart, I knew I had to do the same for someone else one day.

Even though I had made mistakes in my past, I knew God had a plan for my life—a beyond-my-wildest-imagination kind of plan. I knew this because of the way Dannah and Teri (my pastor's wife at the time) believed in me and poured truth into my heart. Before them, I didn't believe any of this to be true. They were my "burning flames" during my high school years. What a powerful testimony! That's the beauty of "passing it on."

Because of what I've been through, I now understand those who've made similar mistakes. I can relate to the heartache, the feelings of hopelessness, worthlessness, and depression. I remember feeling like my heart would never be the same, that the broken pieces of my life could never be put back together. But Dannah taught me the power of perspective, hope, and love by helping me see beyond what I was going through, into a brighter future. Her love and her hope set my heart free! Hope was what I needed and hope is what I received.

One of the greatest gifts we can give to those going through the heartache of sexual sin is HOPE. We may not be able to mend their brokenness, but we can breathe hope and love into the broken places simply by walking alongside of them. Deep friendships are one of the most valuable parts of our lives, but we need the kind of friends we can trust and rely on. The kind of friends who can see all of our junk and pain but love us anyway. I believe all of us are called to be that kind of "burning flame" for someone.

Over the last several years I've had the opportunity to mentor many young girls through the process of healing from sexual sin. Has it been easy? No. Worth it? Yes. I've even had the chance to coach girls through sexual purity and modesty, all because of what I learned as a teenager from Dannah. Since I was once in full-time youth ministry, I've also worked with several teen moms. Their journey is much different than mine, yet the process of healing is the same. Some of them didn't even know Jesus or His unconditional love before I came into their lives. It's incredible what acts of kindness and words of life can do for someone.

Friends, our purpose in life is to love God and love people. We are called to be the hands and feet of Jesus. Our freedom is not just for us but for everyone we meet. If you've been set free and have experienced healing, you walk in an authority that is unique. The kind of authority that triumphs over darkness. The kind of authority that can see captives set free. The kind of authority that can see God's kingdom on earth as it is in heaven.

Imagine a generation filled with the love and hope that comes from Jesus Christ. Imagine a generation whose identity is so founded in who they are in Christ that nothing else matters. Imagine a generation free from sexual perversion and promiscuity. I believe the impossible is possible when we surrender our lives to Him. And I believe that you and I can see this happen in our lifetime, if we're willing to pass it on.

Live life as a burning flame and see a generation impacted for eternity.

Let's go!

Jen Wilton

Jen has served on my Pure Freedom team and is currently in youth ministry and prayer initiatives in Canada.

A Special Letter on Choosing Life

DEAR READER,

I made a mistake. A mistake that I thought was so big that I knew I could never be pure again. But was I ever wrong.

Growing up, every Sunday morning I would put on my freshly pressed Sunday dress, take the rollers out of my hair, and go to church with my family. As I grew older, I began to understand that church wasn't just a tradition that included snacks and music. It was about Jesus who died for me, and I learned to love Him. I was the one in middle school who listened to gospel music instead of heavy metal, followed the rules, and swore I would stay pure until I got married.

Then in high school I started to feel left out. Although I wanted to follow God's commands, I couldn't understand why I felt like I was missing out on so much fun and happiness. Why would God keep me from so much happiness? I gradually stopped going to church and began to date. I thought my boyfriend was perfect. We had our fights, but we liked each other and I was happy.

After a few months, I thought I was ready to break that promise I had made to stay pure. Before long I started to mysteriously gain weight. Thinking I was just eating too much junk food, I started to eat more healthfully and exercise, but no matter how hard I tried I just got bigger, more tired, and more hungry. After lying to my worried boyfriend and my mother, she finally insisted that I take a pregnancy test. It was negative. But the relief was short-lived when Mom took me to the doctor. The doctor, after surmising that I had either cancer or was pregnant, held the Doppler to my stomach. We heard the heartbeat of a healthy, sixth-month preborn baby.

As I lay crying in my room, the questions were overwhelming. *What am I going to do with a baby? How am I going to care for him or her? Should I keep him or her? What was my mom thinking? What would my boyfriend think?* Suddenly my life was turned upside down and that closeness I felt with God as a child seemed further away than ever. How could He love me now?

Landon Garry Park was born a healthy 8lb 5oz. He held my heart in his fingertips. His father never called me back after I had told him that I was pregnant. But my family supported me the best they knew how. Even though I thought my sin was so big it was unforgivable, my older sister brought me to church and also let me tag along on mommy-and-me outings. It was there I met Jen Wilton, a redheaded firecracker who was a youth ministry leader. She was the first stranger I met who didn't judge me once she found out I was a teen mom. As I got to know her, I felt comfortable opening up and sharing my heart with her.

One day Jen invited me into her office and handed me a book. Upon reading the title, I wondered if she was crazy. How could I relate to a book called *The Bride Wore White*? I was dirty. Yes, I knew that Jesus died on the cross for my sins. But my sin was so big, and there was no way I thought I could ever be clean again, much less someday walk down the aisle in a white dress and not be a hypocrite. But I trusted Pastor Jen and opened it.

Through its pages I realized that no matter how terrible I thought my sin was, Jesus died for all of my sins and could make me clean. God forgave me and wanted to be close to me! I found that God still wanted my heart. It wasn't too late to be pure. I was no longer ashamed. And I was no longer embarrassed to dream of finding the man that God had for me because I now knew that I was valued and He wanted the best for me.

So no matter what you have done, it is never too late. Don't draw away from God, He wants to be close to you and make you pure and new once again.

Love,

Tanisha

Tanisha is a member of Jen Wilton's youth group!

A Special Letter on Singleness

DEAR FRIEND,

Singleness is not a disease! It's funny how when you're single in your twenties, you get affirmation and accolades. You're waiting for the right one or focusing on Jesus. Then when you leave the corridor of your twenties, the affirmation wanes and the questions begin to loom. *What's wrong with me? Did I miss the "one"? Maybe if I was more (fill in the blank), I'd be married. Am I supposed to get married? Maybe that's just my desire for my life and not His?* Sound familiar? You're not alone, friend!

Many single women ask those questions, including me! So how do we answer these questions that are laced with fear, doubt, and confusion? Where do we go with the tears of longing, the ache of hope? I know not everyone wants to get married, and I bless those who have answered the call of singleness. For me, even though singleness isn't my call, it *is* my reality right now. In fact, it's been my reality much longer than I ever thought it would.

I had some "checkpoints" in life. I wanted to be married by twenty-five, and I almost reached that goal. But after the pain of a broken engagement, I turned my heart off to the idea of marriage and relationships. (Cliché, right?) I packed up my desires and got lost in the noble work of ministry, but my heart wasn't truly well. After some time, He came and asked me to unpack the desires I had conveniently stored in the compartments of my walled-off heart.

That began a long and painfully beautiful process that continues to this day. He's spoken His promises and brought His encouragement along the way. He told me that marriage is a part of my destiny, and so I wait.

God writes His promises on our hearts, in His Word, and sometimes in other places. At a church in Washington, D.C., a woman whose mother was visiting from Germany asked about the car with the Pennsylvania plate. The woman later told me what her mom said. The first three letters of my license plate, EHE, mean "marriage" in German. God wrote the promise on my license plate. I had been "driving" my promise around! Sometimes His promises are closer than we realize even when we feel like they're far away.

May I share some verses that have held my heart during some very lonely times?

Psalm 126:5: Those who sow in tears will reap with songs of joy. This was my verse as I served my younger and only sister as her maid of honor. My prayer was that on the day of her wedding, I would truly honor and bless her. There were a lot of tears through those months. I was happy for her but hurting for me. I certainly didn't want to be the "spinster sister." I needed His grace, and He came through. On her wedding day, I learned that it is possible to share in someone else's joy!

Isaiah 54:1: "Sing, O barren woman, you who never bore a child; burst into song, shout for joy, you who were never in labor; because more are the children of the desolate woman than of her who has a husband," says the Lord. Sometimes we have to sing over the "barren" places of our lives. One morning, the Lord asked me what word stood out to me the most in that verse. Of course, I said "barren." Here's my English "geekdom" coming out! See, "barren" is the adjective in this sentence. It's a descriptive word. It's not the noun—"woman," which by the nature of the word speaks to the potential of giving birth. It's not the verb—"sing," which is the action word. I was more focused on a description, instead of identity or action. Don't get lost in the descriptions. Singleness is only a description of our lives; it's not our identity, nor is it a word by which we live.

Psalm 37:4: Delight yourself in the Lord and he will give you the desires of your heart. I still believe this. The safest place for my heart is under the umbrella of His delight.

2 Corinthians 1:20: For no matter how many promises God has made, they are "Yes" in Christ. And so through him the "Amen" is spoken by us to the glory of God. He's taught me that His promises are good and true, but they require my agreement—my "amen" or "so be it." At one point in my journey, every night when I went to sleep, I would put my hand on the other side of the bed (and sometimes on my dog, Stuart, who was lying there) and say, "I thank You for the man who will someday lie beside me. I thank You that he loves You even more than he loves me. I thank You that he has a heart of compassion and follows You." (I eventually got bored with calling him "the man" and started making up a new name every night—just for fun.) I've prayed for Fred, Charlie, Jose, Michael . . . the list goes on!

Here are some things that I've learned and am still learning.

Don't contain the tears. Denied tears become hard and contribute to a calloused heart. Let the tears flow when they come. They're an outlet for the longing and the pain. I'm so thankful for my married and single friends who have carried my tears along the way!

Live life! No man can complete you. Only Jesus can. So live your life! Enjoy the benefits that singleness offers us—cereal for dinner, the flexibility to travel, the ability to fully give ourselves to the Lord! Believe it or not, I think that we will miss aspects of our single lives when we eventually get married, so don't miss the beauty of this season!

Don't settle. Wait for His best! (I'm speaking this in real time!) I've had opportunities to date, but have had to say no because I knew in my heart they weren't right for me, or me for them. Growing up, I always felt the need to have a boyfriend. Insecurity drove me to a place where I would avoid being alone. Now, it's been ten years since I've dated, but who's counting? God has taught me that even when I feel lonely, I'm not alone. Don't date for the sake of not being alone. Wait. Wait with me. I believe that He'll make it worth the waiting!

I collect pennies. It's one of the assignments that God gave me. The huge watercooler jug sits in the corner of my bedroom. I don't spend one single penny—haven't in years. When the pennies collect in my car or wallet, I empty them out, carry my "seed" to the jug, release them, and say, "Thank You for the man You're bringing into my life." While most people wouldn't bother to pick up a penny on the ground, I'll just about dive for it! To me, a penny isn't our least valuable coin; it's a symbol of His most valuable promise! Someday, I'll cash those pennies in and that money will go toward buying my husband's wedding band.

Wait with me, okay?

Love,

Stephanie

Stephanie Peters is the worship leader at most of my Pure Freedom events for teens. But she's hard to get because she's in demand as a worship trainer in churches across the world. If you've ever worshiped under her leadership, you know that she changes your heart powerfully. Check out her music and her ministry at heartexposedmusic.com.

(I have contributed to her penny collection!)

NOTES

Chapter Two—Satan's Big Fat Sex Lies
1. CDC Youth risk behavior surveillance—United States, 2009, http://www.cdc.gov/mmwr/pdf/ss/ss5905.pdf , *MMWR* 2010;59(SS-5);p20.
2. Chlamydia, http://www.ncbi.nlm.nih.gov/pubmedhealth/PMH0002321/ , updated June 2010, retrieved October 12, 2011.
3. Genital HPV Fact Sheet, http://www.cdc.gov/std/hpv/stdfact-hpv.htm, updated August 2011, retrieved October 12, 2011.
4. Vinay Kumar, Abul K. Abbas, Nelson Fausto, Richard N. Mitchell, *Robbins Basic Pathology*, 8th edition, Saunders Elsevier, 718–721, retrieved October 12, 2011.
5. Center for Disease Control, HPV and Cervical Cancer: Testimony of Ronald O. Valdiserri, M.D., M.P.H. Deputy Director, CDC's National Center for HIV, STD, and TB Prevention before the Committee on Energy and Commerce Subcommittee on Health, US House of Representatives, 16 March 1999. http://cdc.gov/washington/testimony/wh031699b.htm. Accessed 15 May 2003.

Chapter Three—Satan's Biggest, Fattest Sex Lie
1. Ed Young, *Pure Sex* (Sisters, Oreg.: Multnomah, 1007), 12–13.
2. "More U.S. Youth Say They Are Not Having Sex", http://reuters.com/article/2011/03/03health-sex-teens-idUSN0322320820110303, March 3, 2011, retrieved October 12, 2011.
3. MTV-AP Digital Abuse Study, http://www.athinline.org/about, September 2011, retrieved November 30, 2011.
4. Robert T. Michael, John H. Gagnon, Edward O. Laumann, and Gina Kolata, *Sex in America* (Chicago: Univ. of Chicago Press, 1996), 124–25.
5. Elisabeth Elliot, *Passion and Purity* (Grand Rapids: Revell, 1984), 21.

Chapter Six—Secret #1: Purity Is a Process
1. Kaye Briscoe King, *Journey: Wolfing into Wholeness: Body, Mind and Spirit* (Dallas: Kaye Briscoe King, 1994), 67–68.

Chapter Nine—Secret #3: Purity Is Governed by Its Value
1. Ed Young, *Pure Sex* (Sisters, Oreg.: Multnomah, 1997), 81.
2. Joshua Harris, *I Kissed Dating Goodbye* (Sisters, Oreg.: Multnomah, 1997), 88.
3. This is a widely quoted sentence by Steinem. I retrieved it from brainyquote.com.
4. Ibid., 40–41.
5. Elisabeth Elliot, *Passion and Purity* (Grand Rapids: Revell, 1984), 136.

Chapter Ten—Secret #4: Purity Speaks Boldly
1. Robert Wolgemuth, *She Calls Me Daddy* (Colorado Springs: Focus on the Family Publishing, 1996), 73.
2. Ibid., 62.
3. Elisabeth Elliot, *Passion and Purity* (Grand Rapids: Revell, 1984), 96.

Chapter Twelve—Secret #6: Purity Embraces Wise Guidance
1. David Blankenhorn, *Fatherless America* (New York: Basic Books, 1995), 46.
2. Kristine Napier, *The Power of Abstinence* (New York: Avon Books, 1996), 67.
3. Ibid., 19.
4. Nathalie Bartle, *Venus in Blue Jeans* (Boston: Houghton Mifflin, 1998), 172.
5. Ronald Hutchcraft, *How to Get Your Teenager to Talk to You* (Wheaton, Ill.: Victor, 1984), 50.
6. Napier, *Power of Abstinence*, 9.
7. Bartle, *Venus*, 97.

Chapter Thirteen—The Truth About Sex: It's Out of This World
1. Ed Young, *Pure Sex* (Sisters, Oreg.: Multnomah, 1997), 18.
2. Edwin Louis Cole, *The Glory of Sex* (Tulsa: Honor Books, 1993), 35.
3. Ed and Gaye Wheat, *Intended for Pleasure* (Grand Rapids: Revell, 1977), 53.
4. Ibid, 22.

Chapter Fourteen—The Truth About Sex: Getting Down to Earth
1. Robert J. Levin and Amy Levin, "Sexual Pleasure: The Surprising Preferences in 100,000 Women," *Redbook* 145 (September 1970), 52.
2. Greg Johnson and Susie Shellenberger, *What Hollywood Won't Tell You About Sex, Love, and Dating* (Ventura, Calif.: Regal, 1994), 17–18.
3. Tim and Beverly LaHaye, *The Act of Marriage* (Grand Rapids: Zondervan, 1976), 209.
4. Kristine Napier, *The Power of Abstinence* (New York: Avon Books, 1996), 60–61.

Chapter Sixteen—Secret #7: Purity Watches Burning Flames
1. Kristine Napier, *The Power of Abstinence* (New York: Avon Books, 1996), 89–90.
2. Henry T. Blackaby and Claude V. King, *Experiencing God: Youth Edition* (Nashville: Lifeway Press, 1994), 27.

DANNAH GRESH Presents...

It's not just about purity.
IT'S ABOUT BEAUTY!

Mother daughter time!

Live worship!

The world has been lying to us. It's time for some good truthful girl talk about guys, beauty and modesty. Believe it or not, no one better to talk it over with than mom. Moms and teen daughters will find that out just about the time a friend hits the runway in this season's hottest fashion, or someone wins a round of "Are You Smarter Than Your Hormones?" Pure Freedom is a fast-paced event designed by Dannah Gresh to help you follow the trail of one provocative, ancient word through the Bible to discover just what God has to say about purity, true beauty and modesty!

♡ **Dannah Gresh,**
Best-selling Author,
And the Bride Wore White and
What Are You Waiting For?

♡ **Stephanie Peters,**
Worship Leader

Pure Freedom is from the creator of Secret Keeper Girl!
www.purefreedom.org

SECRET KEEPER

978-0-8024-0253-0   978-0-8024-3977-2

True beauty—the kind that draws people to you-—comes from deep within. It comes from way below the surface. Deeper than your closet. Farther than the mall. Far beyond the corners of fashion magazines. If you want to discover the power of your beauty, you will have to meet the One who created you.

PureFreedom.org

Also available as an ebook

MOODY
PUBLISHERS

www.MoodyPublishers.com

INSPIRING GREATNESS
for
125
YEARS
1887–2012

Cedarville University is a Christ-centered learning community equipping undergraduate, graduate, and online students for lifelong leadership and service through an education marked by excellence and grounded in biblical truth.

Nationally recognized for academic quality, career outcomes, and overall student satisfaction, Cedarville enrolls some of the brightest minds in the nation who are also passionate about accomplishing great things for Jesus Christ.

A Cedarville education, priced affordably and competitively, is an investment in the future. Students living on campus or engaging online are inspired to know God in a deeper way while being prepared to thrive professionally.

**This is Cedarville University ...
inspiring greatness for 125 years.**

Learn more: cedarville.edu

CEDARVILLE
UNIVERSITY.

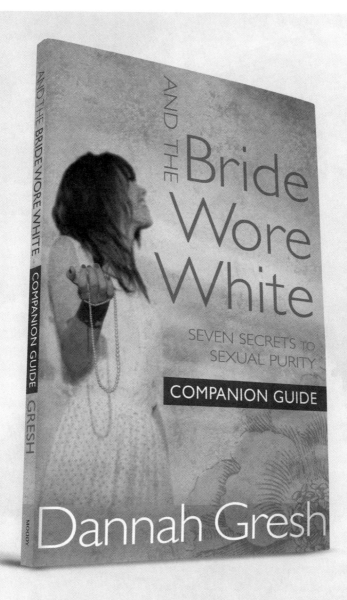

AND THE BRIDE WORE WHITE

COMPANION GUIDE

GRESH

AND THE

Bride
Wore
White

SEVEN SECRETS TO
SEXUAL PURITY

COMPANION GUIDE

Dannah Gresh

MOODY

This journal, a companion guide to be used as you read the bestselling *And the Bride Wore White*, provides fun and thought-provoking activities that will help young women embrace God's design for sexuality and purity. It can be an individual or small group study. Videos and leader guides are available at purefreedom.org.

MOODY
Publishers™

From the Word to Life